Publication Te

MANAGING EDITOR
Elisabeth Tuck – Mt. Diablo
POETRY EDITOR
Anita I. Holmes – High Desert
SUBMISSIONS MANAGER
David George – Mt. Diablo
FORMATTING & DESIGN
Joyce Krieg – Central Coast Writers

PROSE ACQUISITION JUDGES
Inland Empire – Judy Kohnen
Marin – Colleen Rae
Mt. Diablo – Bob Poirier, Dot Edwards, Fran Cain, Heidi
Eliason, Judith Marshall, Marianne Lonsdale, Robin Gigoux,
Susan Berman, Suzi Orpin
Orange County – Jeanette Fratto
Redwood Writers – Mark Piper
South Bay Writers – Dave LaRoche, Jana McBurney-Lin
Tri-Valley Writers – Lani Longshore

POETRY ACQUISITION JUDGES
Berkeley – Keith Gaboury, Richard M. Rocco
Central Coast Writers – Sophia Morency, Tom Rebold, Rags
Rosenberg, C. Jonathan Shoemaker, Steve Wheeler
Fremont Area Writers – Patricia Doyne
High Desert – Lorelei Kay
Orange County – Kristine Rae Anderson
Redwood Writers – Skye Blaine, Les Bernstein, Robin
Gabbert, Fran Claggett-Holland, Marianne Lyon
Sacramento – Charles Bates, Louise Church, Susan Dlugach,
Marcia Ehinger
San Francisco Peninsula – Kate Adams, BEH
San Joaquin Valley – Leslie Liberty
Tri-Valley Writers – Constance Hanstedt

The California Writers Club Story

California Writers Club is a 501(c)3 educational nonprofit corporation founded in 1909 out of the lively literary scene in San Francisco's East Bay region that flourished in the first decade of the 20th century. The CWC incorporated in 1913 and has held meetings for over 100 years.

Today the CWC has nearly 2000 members in 22 branches throughout the state, and remains one of the oldest organizations for writers in continuous operation in the nation.

CWC's mission is to educate members and the public in the craft and business of writing and opens membership to writers of all interests, levels, and genres. Our website, calwriters.org, has specific information about membership and links to the individual branches.

2022-2023 OFFICERS

President – Roger Lubeck, Redwood Writers
Vice-President – Bob Isbill, High Desert
Secretary – Elisabeth Tuck, Mt. Diablo
Treasurer – Constance Hanstedt, Tri-Valley Writers

CALIFORNIA WRITERS CLUB

Literary Review

ISSUE NO. 11 · 2022

CWC PRESS

The California Writers Club Literary Review is published annually by
The California Writers Club, a 501(c)3 nonprofit
P.O. Box 11212
Pleasanton, CA 94588-1212
calwriters.org

ISBN: 978-1-7356372-2-8

California Writers Club Annual Literary Review 2022 – An annual statewide anthology of prose & poetry by our members.

1. American poetry – 21st century

2. American short prose – 21st century

I. Title: California Writers Club Literary Review 2022

II. California Writers Club

Front cover photograph: Jill Hedgecock – Mt. Diablo
Back cover artwork: Linda Loveland Reid –
Redwood Writers

Printed & mailed by BR Printing, San Jose, California

Published by
CWC Press
P.O. Box 11212
Pleasanton, CA 94588-1212

CWC Branches

Berkeley
Central Coast Writers
Coastal Dunes
East Sierra/Ridge Writers
Fremont Area Writers
High Desert
Inland Empire
Long Beach
Marin
Mt. Diablo
Napa Valley Writers
North State Writers
Orange County
Redwood Writers
Sacramento
San Fernando Valley
San Francisco Peninsula
San Joaquin Valley
South Bay Writers
Tri-Valley Writers
Writers of Kern
Writers of the Mendocino Coast

Table of Contents

Prose

ESSAY

MEMOIR

HUMOR

Poetry

Notes from the Editors

ELISABETH TUCK (MT. DIABLO) - PROSE EDITOR
ANITA I. HOLMES (HIGH DESERT) - POETRY WRANGLER

Once again, many thanks to Submissions Manager David George (Mt. Diablo) who logged all submissions, replied to members that their pieces were received, then passed the submissions on for judging.

Elisabeth Tuck (Mount Diablo) returned as managing editor for prose submissions. This year, Anita I. Holmes (High Desert) took on the editor's role for poetry.

The Reader Judges

The *Literary Review* cannot happen without the many dozens of volunteer reader-judges. We want to thank all who read, graded, and wrote feedback. Our goal was that the comments be useful and encouraging.

For prose we especially want to laud Mark Piper of Redwood Writers, a former English teacher, for the huge percentage of prose submissions he read and for which he gave thoughtful, kind, and helpful feedback. If Elisabeth didn't send him a new batch quickly, he reminded her. That was supportive!

Kudos to Lorelei Kay (High Desert), who diligently provided feedback on more than half the poetry submissions. Many of these she emailed while traveling or in the midst of a family move.

The wide range of prose and poetry genres made reading the submissions enjoyable. "I learned so much," was a common comment from this year's first-time reader-judges.

CWC Members

We encourage our members to become involved and continue to help each other to write well. Give each other helpful feedback. Find encouraging writing buddies who will help you grow, too. It can be difficult to do your very best in isolation.

As writers, we know what our scenes are, who the characters are, what the words mean as we've put them together. It can be an eye-opener to share our work and discover whether others see the same thing. So much of our writing development takes place at the branch levels.

Layout and Design

Huge thanks to Joyce Krieg (Central Coast Writers), who has wrestled the *Literary Review* into shape.

To everyone, when you thoroughly *read* and *follow* the guidelines any time you present your work for publication, you grow as a writer and help make the publishing team's job easier.

Thank you all,

Elisabeth and Anita

Foreword

ROGER LUBECK - PRESIDENT, CALIFORNIA WRITERS CLUB

This issue of the California Writers Club *Literary Review* includes more than 30 works of fictions, essay, memoir, and humor. There are more than 40 poems. The member authors in this edition represent twenty-one branches. In my time with the club, I consider this one of the best issues. The stories are meaningful and entertaining. I found myself sitting with other writers in a foreign café, joining a man and his dog on a park bench, and trudging through deep snow. In one story I relived my days watching TV cowboys. In another I experienced the songs of silence. There are stories about families, birds, dogs, Christmas trees, Chanukah, soup kitchens, and kings and queens. There are poems of all types and forms. Emotional poems that explore the nature of being human—love, illness, death, and most of all, being alive. Vivid poetry filled with images of nature, forests, beaches, moonlit nights, horses, vultures, and lava flows.

When you read the poems, essays, memoirs, and stories in this issue, I hope you will appreciate the literary craft of our member authors and recognize the care and quality their writing represents. To all our members, I hope you will take inspiration from this substantial new collection, and I encourage and challenge each of you to continue to hone your craft and seek every avenue this great club provides to see your words in print.

A Night at the Café Verona
HENRI BENSUSSEN - REDWOOD WRITERS

We writers sit under the heat lamps in the small, covered courtyard outside Café Verona, at round, marble-topped tables. Double glass doors open to the café proper. Inside is a long coffee bar and next to it a glass case holding slices of chocolate cakes and cheesecakes, little cream tarts, cupcakes, and lemon bars. We are like the cakes in there, held apart by the glass, kept cool in the night air, waiting for something to happen.

Something always happens, and often what happens is not what other people might call a happening. For us, it's a value-added operation. We take innocuous events—a couple walking in out of the rain, a woman pounding away at a portable typewriter at a table in the corner, a man sitting at the bar watching the waiter, who wears a silver earring in each ear—and make of them engrossing experiences, exquisite moments, bon-bons for the heart.

At Café Verona the espresso is robust, the cappuccino artistically presented, and even a plain coffee is served in a china cup. The atmosphere is quiet and well lit for those who like to read alone. As writers we welcome the chance to overhear conversations. The courtyard is a few feet away from the sidewalk and street. Steady traffic. It is raining, as it has for what seems like months. We are ready for the rain to stop. Our writing runs down the page like raindrops sliding down a window. Ours is a steady rain of words.

Four older men enter the café. They inspect the offerings in the glass case, and wander to a nearby table where they can continue their inspection. They would like to order a dessert, but all that sugar, butter, and cream might make their blood race. A slice of cheesecake? Better to imagine the taste of it, the texture on the tongue.

Waiters push the chairs across the red-tiled floor. More people are coming out the glass doors than entering. Everyone carries an umbrella. The woman at the typewriter prepares to leave. She puts her papers in her satchel and snaps the typewriter into its case. I label her a journalist, but another writer says she's more likely a grad student from the university. She has wavy red hair, and wears a pink sweater. She is either planning to meet her boyfriend, or she will seduce a stranger instead. I'm, basically, a writer of romances, rather than of *belle lettres*, which is a word I learned at a conference in New York. I find myself often imagining different ways to pronounce it.

The four men are standing now at the glass case, pointing. Baba au rhum they've decided is worth the loss of a small slice of life. Our lives feel enmeshed with theirs through the payment of our attention. They drink bitter espressos that remind them of the place they remember as home without being home anymore. We savor the flavor and smokiness of rum as it combines with lemon, slips down the waiting throat, we who have not been anywhere but here.

Time passes. We put away pens, say our goodbyes, and rush to our cars. The man at the bar is still there. The waiter with the earrings cleans around the bar, washes glasses, lingers by the man long enough to stroke his hand before wiping down the space that minutes ago held a glass of ale, a plate with a slice of cake. The two leave together. The lights are off. In the dark they kiss, disappear into the rain arm in arm. Later each will arrive home, having studied late at the library, they say, to sleep with their partners.

Dad's Ashes

KAREN C. UPHOFF - WRITERS OF THE MENDOCINO COAST

the weight of them, a reduction of
skin, bones, organs and metal parts,
     neatly packaged
a plastic bag, zip-tied
in plastic box—grey
to match our mood

his heart, the weight of it,
not included here
     so buoyant,

it never tipped the scale
against the feather of Maat, the truth of that
tucked in my heart,
     with his smile
his granite belief in who I am,
that life is worth living (and usually funny)

each day, without
        him—darkened
with heavy clouds hauled by crows,
that scatter rain, ash
clinker
        of memories
landing like dust
on everything,
        we touch
and touched us.

Good Attitude Is Everything

JEANNE RANA - BERKELEY

Good attitude is everything
No gain in being negative
Getting old is not much fun
I tell myself that all is well

No gain in being negative
I concentrate on what still works
I tell myself that I'm all right
I pray for patience, clarity

I concentrate on what still works
my eyes, my lungs, my heart, my feet
I pray for patience, clarity
when I forget to do something

My eyes, my lungs, my heart, my feet
I am careful every day
When I forget to do something
I laugh a bit instead of curse

I am careful every day
I find adventures on my walk
I laugh a bit instead of curse
when I lose my phone, my purse

I find adventures on my walk
at the market, in the park
When I lose my phone, my purse
I stop and wait, then look again

at the market, in the park
Getting old is not much fun
I stop and wait, then look again
Good attitude is everything

Revelations

LINDA MUTTY - CENTRAL COAST WRITERS

Never revealed she suspects malfunction
Loved ones kept in semi darkness
Endure sudden flares extinguished
As suddenly as they appear

She never lands for long
Like a small bird
Momentarily alert, watchful
Taking flight to safer harbor

She thinks she can
She tries so hard
Her words come forth
Stumbling, searching for meaning

She knows my name but doesn't
A sister unrecognized by name
Yet, within she knows me
Seventy years of life connect us

It has stolen a part of her
This one most recent
How many in the past?
We are told many

Revelations slowly appear
In sterile quarters from strangers
    Four days pass then discharged
A chair rolls her to us

Her heart, her heart, her heart
They tell us this
    Results will confirm
    Heart strokes

Damaged, broken
In need of repair
Damaged and broken
Her heart, her heart, her heart

Another breath taken she survives
Thriving on others' concerns
Surrounding herself in their concerns
Drowning in their weight

Uninvited, unexpected revelations
    Seventy years of damage done
Her heart, her heart, her heart
So little time left to heal

A Walk along the Levees
PATRICIA COLLINS - SOUTH BAY WRITERS

On a typical January day, only a few minutes' drive from a packed population of apartment and townhouse dwellers, resident and migratory birds—ruddy ducks, mallards, northern shovelers, teals, and gadwalls—float amidst ponds and along the southern San Francisco Bay's Charleston Slough. Male and female pairs paddle toward a shoreline or simply take a meandering path in the water. American coots—easy to spot with their black bodies and white beaks—float among their distant genetic relatives. Even more distinctive are the common gallinules, whose bright red bills are tipped with yellow and whose legs are lime green. I cannot imagine why their name includes "common."

From the grassy banks of the channels, snowy egrets and great blue herons keep one watchful eye on human passersby; great egrets take to graceful flight. Large ravens stand their ground along the trailside with a don't-you-dare bully's stare. White-tailed kites and peregrine falcons soar above in search for prey. Turkey vultures soar low and search for carrion. A stretch of a levee is blanketed with white pelicans.

This is an ecosystem that appears to thrive on tolerance. The coots weave through a flotilla of mallards without so much as a skirmish. The raptors have the same goal, and it's not each other's demise. The cormorants look down from their perch on a high-voltage electrical tower with seeming disinterest in what's happening below and above.

Each time I walk there—often for as long as two hours—I am heartened by my ability to focus on all of this natural wonder and to forget about the man-made structures just beyond this shoreline, artifacts of the region's dense human population: a far-reaching water pollution control facility, towering landfill mounds, and a string of high-voltage power lines that span this end of the Bay. Along the water's edge, a Lockheed-Martin campus, Moffett Airfield, Shoreline Amphitheater, and, to the south, high-rise office buildings assert another kind of power.

But look beyond them and the Santa Cruz Range appears to the west. Look north along that ridge to see fingers of white fog over shallow gaps. Think back on the history of this area while walking past a salt pond—one that remains of the many that were part of a booming salt industry before California became part of the United States, before the discovery of California gold.

Eastward, across the bay, the Diablo Range begins its winding path that reaches all the way south to Salinas. The Lick Observatory is visible, perched on Mount Hamilton as if it were observing the valley and not the universe beyond our planet. The hillsides' native grasses have changed from gold to green, marking the season's change in this peculiar land where rain falls from mid-autumn to mid-spring, only to yield to month after month of bold sun and dry air.

The term "barrenness of winter" has no place here; it is winter's natural bounty that thrives.

Song of Exaltation
MARK MEIERDING - REDWOOD WRITERS

Let us praise the lace and muscles of this universe,
and thank the flailing runner falling from his race;
praise petitions lingering on the widow's face.
Extol the long monotonies
of the depot's wooden bench
and dreams that flee from fire escapes.

Praise the universe for sharps and flats
and the conjugation of saxophones,
for lemon curd and naked light upon the rose,
for parabolic arcs and rhyme
that's deafening as empty choir lofts.
For hards and the scorching softs, praise,
as they twist and taste and chafe
together in their haste.

For temples and decay, praise.
For sellers of salvation, the cheerleaders,
the shiny hucksters and all cheaters, too;
for paprika, nasturtiums—and teeth.

Praise toddlers' fears of night
and bitter men's forgiven debts.
Honor ashes and unopened quilts and the labyrinth.
Praise this, our universe, for silence and for snails
and obstacles between the verbs.
Praise bellowing kine, dead swords, and rust,
promised serpents and braided trust,
wild doors that open to our drums' device.
Now let us praise this
sacred paradise.

Canticle

SIMONA CARINI - REDWOOD WRITERS

Connect me to your roots.
Far from columned cathedrals
I entered the forest's shade.
Redwoods rose, dark pillars,
beyond my gaze's reach.

I will travel with the sap
to the top, see marbled murrelets
and salamanders at home
in your canopy, ferns
and huckleberries growing
up above, cloistered
from their kind on the ground.

Sunlight filtered through the canopy
as through mullioned windows
to the umber ground
soft with layered leaves,
shone on my steps,
the nave lined with ferns,
patches of sorrel deep green
and burgundy, like a rich carpet.
A varied thrush whistled.

Teach me to reach the scared,
the fire-scarred, the faces
with spent gazes.

In the airy space, redwoods
listened to my words, held them
in the light, grains of soil,
offered them back to me.

Bench of the Beloved
JIM HASSE - MT. DIABLO

In the spring, I first saw them—a man and his dog. As I climbed up the grassy hill to the stately heritage oak, I stopped at the bench beneath it to catch my breath. There they sat as if expecting me.

"We thought maybe you'd come today," the man said. "Greetings. I'm Harvey, and this is Millie."

"Hi, I'm Jay." I smiled and nodded. I almost asked what he meant by his comment, but I didn't. "Is this your bench?"

"Why, yes, whenever we're here. When we're not, anyone can use it." He laughed.

Harvey looked to be in his mid-eighties, and Millie seemed to be about the same age, in dog years, that is. Harvey was thin but fit-looking. He had a full head of light gray hair and didn't wear glasses or a hearing aid. He was casually dressed in a light green polo shirt and khaki trousers. It would have been quite natural if he had been sitting there holding a glass of chardonnay. I immediately liked him.

Millie had a smooth, dark brown coat. She looked to be a cross between a chocolate lab and a rottweiler. She had a sturdy build with a stubby, docked tail. The gray around her muzzle hinted at her vintage age. She sat calmly, keeping steady eye contact with me. Her soulful, brown eyes seemed to say, "I understand everything you say."

"Hello, Millie," I said, slowly extending my hand to her. She sniffed, but didn't lick. She had nothing more to say to me.

Harvey slid to the side of the bench, making room for me. "Oh, no thanks, Harvey, I need to keep going. Definitely another time." He smiled. I had recently taken up walking and was intent on getting in six or eight miles every day. The weather was warming up, and the rolling hills urged me on. I wished my new acquaintances well and waved as I headed over the ridge to the valley.

I walked along the back route by the "oak tree bench" with Harvey and Millie twice a day. I usually walked between 10:00 a.m. and 1:00 p.m., and soon, we began to see each other regularly. Occasionally I just waved as I walked past, but most often, I stopped to join them.

Harvey and I skipped the usual small talk—where we lived, what we had done for a living, our current hobby, or our plans for the immediate future. Instead, we shared our observations and thoughts about the nature around us—the grasses and trees, the hawks above, and recent coyote sightings. We pretty much stayed in the moment and sometimes even sat quietly for five or ten minutes taking in the inspiring view of majestic Mount Diablo, robed in spring-green grasses. Every time I saw my new friends, I felt a lift in my step and in my spirit.

Spring came and went. The hills turned golden. I kept up my walking routine, and my friends and I kept meeting at the bench. Harvey started wearing a tan Panama hat, and I wore a University of Alabama baseball cap. The hot summer sun dictated our new head coverings. I had switched from jeans to shorts, but Harvey continued to wear casual slacks. I wore T-shirts, and Harvey wore short sleeve cotton shirts. He wore sturdy walking shoes, and I wore Nike running shoes.

In late August, I crested the hill and saw Millie sitting alone on the bench. I looked around for Harvey, but he was nowhere in sight. Thinking something might be wrong, I waited around for ten minutes but finally concluded they were okay and went on my way. I told myself that I'll check on Millie when I return in forty minutes. But when I came back, the dog was gone, and still no Harvey.

Two days later, I was glad to see man and dog together again on the bench. I joined them but said nothing about Harvey's absence. As the days went by, I noticed that Harvey seemed to be losing weight. I asked him about it.

He said casually, "I have kidney problems and have been sick lately. And yes, Jay, you're right, I have lost weight. This is all natural, though. This is just what happens." He seemed calm and emotionally unaffected by his condition.

I said, "Is it possible Millie has lost some weight, too?"

"Good observation. Yes, she has lost some weight. She has kidney problems, too." He then casually repeated what he had just said regarding himself, "This is all natural. It's just what happens." Harvey would never mention their illness again, and I wouldn't ask.

"If there is anything I can do, Harvey, let me know."

"Thanks. I will." I stood up, patted him on the shoulder, and hit the trail again, but I couldn't shake my concern for them.

As the weather began to cool, I went back to wearing jeans and long-sleeve T-shirts. Harvey resumed wearing long-sleeve shirts and a sweater or a light jacket. Both man and dog looked even thinner and frail. I wanted to pat Millie, but I thought she was too dignified for that.

At the end of September, I again found Millie sitting alone on the bench, this time for two days in a row. On the third day, she jumped down and beckoned me to follow her. I did. I watched her walk up to the front door of a small white clapboard house with dark green shutters. She scratched twice. The door opened, and in she went. I stood staring at the house for a moment, surprised that Harvey and Millie lived only a few blocks from me. I couldn't believe our paths had never crossed until we met at the old oak tree on the hill.

I went up to the door and rang the bell. A pleasant-looking woman in her early eighties opened the door and said, "Yes. Can I help you?"

"I'm Jay, a friend of Harvey and Millie," I said. "We used to meet almost every day at the bench on the top of the hill. I haven't seen Harvey for a while. Is he okay?"

The woman smiled warmly at me. "Nice to meet you, Jay. I'm Harvey's sister, Alice. I've heard about you." She paused. "Well, he's been sick and hasn't felt much like walking. Millie has been going up to the bench, and when she returns, they spend time together. I think she keeps him up to date on what's going on up there." She smiled again and winked.

"Do you think he would want a visitor?" I asked.

"Well," she hesitated again. "He is in hospice care now and seems to be enjoying the quiet. I'll tell him you asked after him."

"Thanks. Please tell him I said it has been a pleasure." Sadness filled my heart.

"Oh, I sure will." Alice had the same peaceful demeanor as her brother.

For the next week, I saw Millie twice a day on the bench, once on the way over the hill and once coming back. I sensed she was keeping vigil. On Friday, I sat down next to her. She met my gaze, got up, scooted closer to me, and laid her head down on my lap. I felt a lump in my throat as I fought back my tears. The normally reserved, impersonal Millie I had come to know never did anything like that before. She released a big sigh and then licked the back of my hand several times. I gently stroked her head. After a few minutes, she got up, jumped from the bench, and slowly walked down the steep hill. I followed her back to Harvey's house. From the street I watched her scratch at the front door twice. The door opened, and she walked in.

The following day Millie wasn't there. I had trouble sleeping that night and dreamed about the man and the dog who had become my friends. As we gathered, Harvey told me: "This is the 'Bench of the Beloved.' It is a sacred place. Words have no value here. Sit and be at peace." Millie sat beside him, looking as if she were smiling in agreement.

When I woke in the morning, I quickly dressed and ate breakfast, excited to get up to the bench as soon as possible. Something seemed to be pulling me there. I hoped to see Millie, and for that matter, Harvey too. Wouldn't that be something? Oh, to see Harvey well again. I sprinted up the hill anticipating a happy reunion. But when I reached the bench, it was empty. No Millie, no Harvey. Disappointed, I kept walking over the hill and then back. My shoulders sagged as I sat on the bench. But recalling the times my friends and I had sat here together, a deep peace welled up inside me.

After an hour, I strolled down to Harvey's house and rang the doorbell. Alice opened the door. I said, "Is everything okay?"

"Life is full of changes," she said serenely. "How are you, Jay?"

"Uh, I'm fine," I said, stumbling over my words. "I haven't seen Millie for a couple of days." I wasn't sure I wanted to hear any more. Alice stepped onto the porch.

"Harvey passed away yesterday afternoon at four o'clock."

My stomach tightened. "I am so sorry, Alice." She smiled at me and continued.

"Harvey had been in the hospital for the past three days. While he was gone, Millie would lie on the rug beside his bed for hours. After lunch yesterday, I called her several times to let her out, but she wouldn't get up. Then I got the call telling me that Harvey had died. I went into his room and saw Millie lying there peacefully. I put my hand on her side and could tell she, too, had died. Quite a coincidence, huh?"

A tear escaped from my eye. I didn't know what to say. I finally hugged Alice and choked out, "Thank you."

In the days that followed, I knew what I wanted to do for my dear friends, Harvey and Millie. If you ever visit the bench under the old oak tree on the hill, you'll see a small brass plate on the top slat declaring: "This is the Bench of the Beloved. It is a sacred place. Words have no value here. Sit and be at peace."

Preparing Soup

MARIANNE BREMS - SAN FRANCISCO PENINSULA

It's the attachment of new shelves
on empty walls that helps absorb the acid of grief,
surfaces to hold familiar vases, books, and photographs
along with new ones.

She removes these things from confinement
in boxes she will soon flatten,
places them in the space bound to shrink
as her collection regrows in her new condo.

There are cabinet shelves to cover, curtains to hang,
hooks to secure,
and still so many boxes, more than she remembers
though she left so much behind.

Focus falters as her dog stares at her from next to his dish.
Without urgency, she squeezes and releases
the loose folds of skin behind his ears,
squeezes and releases, before filling his bowl.

He retrieves from the bedroom the red plaid flannel shirt
she gave her husband of forty-one years
last Christmas before the accident.
The dog jumps into her lap, plaid between his teeth.

She takes her time spreading the shirt over them both,
smoothing each fold as they lock eyes for a moment.
Heavy with fatigue and the slow drip of grief,
she hangs the shirt over the back of one dining room chair
and carefully buttons each button down the front.

She can see it there beside the table
as darkness gathers outside the curtainless window
and she prepares soup.

We
(after "Design" by Robert Frost)
RAGS ROSENBERG - CENTRAL COAST WRITERS

You hum a quiet tune behind your screen,
I sip my coffee, scroll from left to right.
You think in ones and zeroes, byte by byte,
I do not speak the language of machine.
And yet we are binary, it seems,
welded together in this bluish light,
swimming late into this sleepless night
through endless pages in the data stream.
What force of nature in the name of fate
brought blood-rich vein and half-a-mile of wire
into a symbiosis to create
for want, or need, this unlikely mate?
And from this coupling what is to be sired,
as yet unknown, but secretly desired?

Christmas Storm Trek

ROD MORGAN - REDWOOD WRITERS

The blizzard howled its challenge and offered a choice. Fix a warm satisfying beverage, swaddle myself in cozy attire, retreat to the La-Z-Boy, and spend the evening mesmerized by dancing flames in the hearth while drifting in and out of a peaceful slumber. I chose the opposite. Urged on by the echoes of ancestral Danish Vikings, I bundled up in warm, waterproof layers of cold-weather gear to venture out into the fray for an arduous trek, walking the storm.

This was an endeavor best faced slightly numb and a wee bit whiskey bent. One hand cinched the fur-lined ear flaps tight while the other raised the bottle of Canadian VO. I downed a measured draw to steel my resolve, but not enough to add the peril of drunkenness. Stepping past the protection of the solid wooden door, I was smacked with the bite of frigid night air, the kind that freezes your exhaled condensation into icicles on your mustache and/or wooly muffler. Snowflakes, the huge, wet kind, were propelled across my face by a blast of icy wind.

The alcohol began to surge into my bloodstream as I turned into the stiff breeze and started down the sidewalk. For twenty minutes I trudged against the fury with robust vigor. The tempest ebbed and grudgingly relinquished its dark cloak to a smattering of slate gray clouds playing hide-n-seek with a bright shimmering moon. It was now a luminous and tranquil night. Warmed by the fast pace, I slowed down to immerse myself in appreciation of the surrounding conditions.

Before me lay an imposing winter environment, composed as only nature can accomplish. Mother Earth revealed her stark beauty as I tramped through the carpet of freshly fallen snow. Every windward surface was plastered with a layer of glinting, frozen sleet. The air sparkled with an abundance of microscopic ice crystals. I marveled at the way she dampened the air and muffled every sound while the frosty white blanket amplified every bit of light. The boughs of a juvenile Douglas fir sagged with globs of snow. Underneath, hundreds of red and green Christmas lights glowed softly. The display continued with blue lights draped over a fifty-foot-long hedgerow.

The crusted, crunchy mantle glistened in the evolving light. The illumination created an otherworldly landscape of almost celestial quality. Although exquisitely beautiful, it was just too darn cold to be heaven, because heaven won't kill you. I could sense death beckon a little louder with each degree below freezing.

When my buzz began to wane, I turned and headed home. First, I stomped out a twenty foot Peace Sign in a church parking lot. Then, feeling whimsical, I thought it would be fun to emulate little Billy from the *Family Circus* cartoon. With shuffled steps, I looped around trees, hopped over bushes, zigzagged through the park and playground, leaving behind a meandering, rutted path throughout the neighborhood. Arriving back home, I was fully ready to kick back and enjoy the mellow, warm beverage, La-Z-Boy experience.

Origami

JUNE KINO CULLEN- INLAND EMPIRE

Paper holds memory,
remembers each crimp
and fold. A warm touch
smooths, soothes, opens
to the time it lived in trees.
Gazed upon horizons
unfolding to amber. Watched
the angle of birds in flight.
Drank with midnight silhouettes
lined at the river's edge.

The time has passed
for cluttered selves
weighed by a thousand
pleated cranes. Extend,
release them home
to the moist forest floor
where autumn leaves rest
their heads against the soil,
sleep with the seeds.
Wait for petals to unfurl.

Time

RAGS ROSENBERG - CENTRAL COAST WRITERS

Once upon a time,
When there was still plenty of the stuff,
Before we strapped it to our wrists,

Before it told us
When to sleep and when to wake,
Before all of that,

Before it measured
Our lives with candles on cakes,
Before it could be wasted,

Before it could be suspended
Or given to a friend,
Before it became something we could make,

Before it was used to heal all wounds,
Before you could have a good one
Or a bad one,

Before it invented the future and the past,
Before it was fast or slow, early or late,
Yeah, before all of that:

We just hung out on Chauncey's front porch
On lazy, yellow afternoons
Watching the old men play checkers.

We hiked to the top of Lookout Mountain,
Looked out over the simple homes
And reveled in the lack of progress.

No one knows exactly what happened.
Some say time got bored
or was captured by our imagination

and put to work
So it could earn its keep
Like everyone else.

No one ever thought
It would learn to fly,
But by then, there was no stopping it.

Citizenship

LALLY PIA - SACRAMENTO

Still consumed with the profound emotion that hit when I saw the Liberty Bell, I waited in a long, polished hallway, knees knocking together with dozens of other nervous applicants. Their faces ranged in hue from the snowiest white to ebony black. After what seemed like an eternity, a uniformed bailiff opened a door to usher us into a courtroom. An elderly black-frocked Caucasian judge with a deadpan expression presided behind a raised podium. The early morning light shone through tall windows and skipping dust particles, to illuminate a magnificent American flag that stood beside him. The oak trees outside were decked in their brightest green finery for the occasion. Leaves danced in exultation, which mirrored the skipping rhythm of my own heart.

We shuffled around, a few nervous coughs and muffled whispers contributing to the tension. I caught a whiff of Old Spice. Beside me, an older Hispanic man with weathered hands fiddled with the top button of his impeccable navy blue suit. Cracked, blackened fingernails occasionally reached up to brush tears from the side of his face, which made tears arise in my own eyes.

I looked away, guilty that I'd intruded on his emotional journey, but fully embracing the camaraderie with a stranger whose nervous exultation seemed to match my own. What was his story, I wondered? Might it have been as tortuous as my own? The bailiff shut the door, and moved to stand beside the judge, and it became eerily quiet. In this hush of anticipation, my palms began to sweat. The momentous nature of the step I was about to take made my temples pound to match the erratic rhythm of my heart.

I was overcome with gratitude. Gratitude for all the blessings this wonderful country had already showered on me. In just a few moments I would join my siblings and parents in our commitment to this land that had become our home. The oak leaves still swayed outside in delight. I imagined palm fronds waving at me from Sri Lanka, and a delicate shower of fragrant pink and white frangipani blossoms falling on my shoulders in Ghana to herald this final step.

How far away those countries seemed now. Tears pricked at my eyes. What I'd absorbed from both countries would always be an integral part of who I was, but America had captured my soul. Standing in those shafts of slanted sunlight, we faced the glorious flag, placed our hands on our hearts, and recited the pledge of allegiance. My heart threatened to burst out of my body, and I wanted to scream out my sheer exultation. I imagined that Liberty Bell triumphantly pealing out to proclaim to the world that an American citizen had joined its ranks. And just as suddenly, a deep yearning flowered within me, seemingly coming out of thin air. It reverberated within my body, shocking me with its intensity.

I want to be free.

Nose Job

ROBIN GABBERT - REDWOOD WRITERS

I was the serious big sister.
There for support. You—

Smiling, always smiling,
unworried during pre-op prep.

The wait while you were under dragged on....
I stared at the wallpaper, tongue depressor beige.

Paging through fashion magazines
in the waiting room, I

kept wondering—did you *really* need rhinoplasty?

Yes, your nose was a little
crooked, not unlike mine.

When you came back, you were
not smiling. White gauze bandages

cocooned your face. There was purple
and black swelling where your eyes

had been. The room seemed hot,
the walls melting. Nausea

like morning sickness swept me.
I wasn't pregnant.

Then I was on the floor.
Later I drove you home.

You slept sitting up on the couch.
Your head a thundercloud—

dark shadows with occasional
showers, or rather, leakage.

I slept on the floor beside you
suppressing my own storm.

We were once wild horses

WINDFLOWER - WRITERS OF THE MENDOCINO COAST

I.

We moved
as if the ground was sky
painted in the blush of spring
and our feet a cloud.
We saw stars hanging on trees
felt rain filling the spaces
between bones.

II.

Now we sense the pull of ropes
taking us from wide open plains
into corrals caked with mud.
Will the hooves of our desires
keep galloping over hilltops
across rivers against the wind?
Or will they become nothing more
than echoes forcing
us to put ears to the ground
in the middle of the night
listening
for what was once songs
lulling us to sleep?

III.

How do we turn back
the covers of time
fold them inside out
run our fingertips against
their graying hem
and change them
again, to the color of sky?

Landings
MARK MEIERDING - REDWOOD WRITERS

The plane bellied low against the tarmac,
a barrel of immensity, while passengers
felt, in those few seconds before the embrace,
the snapping back of gravity
in an impossible machine.

Then the vibrating, loud wait of deceleration,
as if one's breath had been tied up
in a brown bag by a dangling ribbon.

The left brain, during landings,
accumulates all past successes, and reassures;
the right remembers once
the shooting stars of wrapped candies
out of an ebullient piñata,
blown apart.

Hairpiece

TRACY NEIS - ORANGE COUNTY

The lady at the wig store was very nice. I suppose that should have come as no surprise. She had been selling hairpieces to cancer patients for more than a decade, after all. But this was my first time interacting with such a shopkeeper, so her gentle manner was much appreciated.

I'd taken my four daughters with me to the store for moral support. And perhaps, I'll admit now, I also brought them along hoping this unwished-for shopping excursion would somehow turn into a fun "girls' day out." Women are supposed to bond over matters of hair, aren't we?

With the help of the shopkeeper and my girls, I selected a shoulder-length, dirty blonde wig with sweeping bangs. The fake hair was nearly the same color as my natural shade, but the bangs would be a new look for me. I'd worn my hair long and straight and bangs-free since I was in third grade (back in the early 1970s). But I hoped the wig's bangs might make my new artificial hairline look more natural.

When I returned home from the store, I placed the wig on its Styrofoam headrest and rested it on top of my dresser. Then I waited for my hair to fall out. That didn't take long. The shopkeeper had told me most of her clients started losing their hair after their third chemotherapy treatment, but I started shedding mine after my second. I handed a pair of scissors to my daughter Karen and asked her to trim my hair into a chin-length bob, so my transition into baldness would not be as traumatic. And then, over the next week, clump by clump, my hair fell out.

Not all of my hair deserted me, however. A few rogue strands clung fiercely to my scalp, giving me a new do that called to mind *The Rocky Horror Picture Show's* Riff Raff on a bad hair day.

Every morning for the next several months, when I glimpsed my reflection in the mirror, I considered slipping on my new wig. But each day I resisted, and instead popped on one of the beanies my daughter Laura had crocheted for me. I knew Laura had crafted each piece with a heart filled with love, and I sensed her affection every time I placed one of her hats on top of my head.

When Laura was in middle school, she sang in a show choir and was required to wear a clip-on, curly ponytail hairpiece that matched those of her fellow altos and sopranos. She hated the damned thing and nicknamed it – not affectionately – "Foofoo." I considered naming my wig too, but I never got around to it. I just stared at it when I lay in bed, recovering from my last bout of chemo, from my painful mastectomy, from my endless rounds of radiation, and I marveled at its uncanny presence on my dresser top. It didn't belong there, beside my jewelry box filled with sentimental treasures and my wicker basket filled with hair ties and barrettes. But I left it there throughout my long months of treatment. Somehow, just seeing it every day reminded me that I could fake normalcy any time I wanted. I could pop that wig on my hairless head and walk into the world without revealing to everyone who saw me that I was a cancer patient. And that, somehow, gave me a strange sense of comfort.

I thought I would have been much more traumatized when my hair fell out. I remember being horrified when I read about the students of Lowood Institute having their curls cruelly chopped off in *Jane Eyre*. And the first time I read *Little Women,* Jo March's sacrificial haircut affected me far more profoundly than her breakup with Laurie ever did. Yet here I was, sacrificing my own "crowning glory," without my consent or desire, and somehow I just took the loss in stride.

Perhaps it was the drugs I was taking. On top of the powerful cocktail of poisons I was receiving each month through my chemotherapy, I was regularly ingesting an industrial-strength anti-nausea pill which set my mind reeling and made me feel like I was floating through life in an out-of-body trance. Most of the time, I hardly even noticed that I was bald.

Or maybe it was the reality of cancer that kept me from mourning my absent hair. I'd lost one of my best childhood friends and a dear college classmate to breast cancer over the last decade. Just thinking of Mary and Colleen kept my perspective in check. My bare head paled in comparison to their deaths.

But looking back on my brush with cancer now, I realize that the wig itself also played a large part in keeping my spirits up. It sat on top of a faceless, head-shaped hunk of white Styrofoam, looking for all the world like a lifeless android prototype that a sci-fi heroine might stumble upon towards the end of a movie. And once that heroine discovers the android's lifeless head, she invariably starts re-evaluating her fellow characters to determine which are real and which are artificial life forms.

My wig was clearly artificial, but each time I looked at it, it reminded me that I, in all my bare-headed glory, was real and alive, and, by God, still breathing. And because it unwittingly bestowed this gift upon me, I will always be grateful to my insentient wig.

It's been almost four years now since I finished my cancer treatment. My re-sprouted eyebrows are much patchier than they used to be, and my eyelashes remain stubbornly at bay. But the hair on top of my head has all grown back. The only real reminder I have of my hairless days is my passport photo, in which I proudly sport a crew cut.

My wig and its Styrofoam headrest have been banished to a high shelf in the back corner of my closet. I've offered the hairpiece to my cosplay-loving daughters to incorporate into a potential costume, but so far they have declined to do so. I think the very notion of wearing my "cancer wig" freaks them out a little.

So there it lies, hidden from public view, covered in a dusty plastic bag. Unlike Foofoo, my wig has remained nameless. I've considered throwing it away or donating it to a cancer ward. But I know I will always be at risk for a recurrence of cancer. So I will keep my wig, perched atop its pale, blank-faced, decapitated, head-shaped form. I never wore it on my head, save that one time I tried it on at the wig store. But it has, nevertheless, grown on me.

Heroes

PHYLLIS M. BUTCHER - SAN FERNANDO VALLEY

My shoulders slumped when I walked into the house and saw the look on my mother's face: we were moving again. Aunt Ruby had found a new place for us to live, this time in Northern California.

"Everyone calls it 'God's Country' up there!" Ruby said, beaming. My grandfather would go on ahead to meet us. He didn't look up from where he was sitting on the sofa.

I hated the idea of another new school, but I was almost ten, and by this time, I knew we never seemed to have a choice. With my four-year-old sister, Kathy, I would go wherever and whenever my mother could find a safe harbor for the three of us. That thing about "God's Country" bothered me, though. If there was any "country" that God owned I assumed it was Heaven, but to the best of my knowledge only dead people lived there. And just the good ones.

Our destination was Auburn, an early gold rush town thirty-six miles east of Sacramento, population about 4,600. The four-hundred-mile trip from Los Angeles in my aunt's 1934 Ford was brutal, inching our way over the two-lane Ridge Route and sweating through sweltering central California. It was well past midnight when we finally bounced over some creaking wooden planks into a yard. The faint outline of a house was visible, and a weak light shone through a window. Otherwise it was pitch black. There would be many things to discover in the morning. And many surprises.

It was 1948, but except for electricity, our new home was devoid of any other modern conveniences. There was a coal-and-wood-burning stove for cooking and heat, and no running water. What served as the bathroom was a sagging structure with an uneven flat roof located outside, about ten yards from the back door. The narrow path leading to it was a minefield of dirt clods and stones. Nighttime trips would not be for the faint hearted. Aunt Ruby evidently had not considered indoor plumbing a high priority when she purchased the property. I watched my mother look around, absorbing what was in store for us. I knew she was devastated, but as always she put up a valiant front for her kids. My hero.

The next morning I stepped outside and surveyed the scene in the light of day. Black tar paper covered the exterior of the house, which explained why it was virtually imperceptible at night. What would pass as a yard was an apron of reddish-brown dirt bordered by sporadic tangles of wild blackberry brambles. A well with a hand pump stood sentry several feet from the front porch. The shaky strips of timber we had driven over the night before spanned a narrow creek with swiftly moving water bouncing lustily over the rocks. It didn't take long for those surroundings to make an irresistible connection with my vivid imagination. All of my Saturday afternoons at the movies, where I would join forces with Hopalong Cassidy, Gene Autry, and the Lone Ranger in their fearless pursuits of justice, could now become a reality. What lay before me was the perfect backdrop to transport me back to the days of yesteryear, of cowboys and Indians, git along little doggies, and the wild, wild West. I thought I had indeed died and gone to Heaven.

Most of my days in God's Country began the same way. I put on my jeans and plaid flannel shirt, my authentic Roy Rogers boots with the plastic spurs, and the revered ten-gallon hat that my mother had miraculously found in a thrift store. Then I headed for the imaginary barn to saddle up my imaginary horse. Her name was "Stormy." Clutching the reins in one hand, I'd urge her out with a few well-rehearsed "clicks" and "clucks" from the corner of my mouth. With my other hand gently slapping her flanks (my thighs) we'd gallop off into the morning. In my head I had already scripted the day's adventure, and if the plot called for a sidekick, I would have to enlist my sweet sister who would gamely gallop along with me until her little legs gave out. All of those magical hours more than compensated for the reality that awaited us at day's end: no warm bath and no putting off the dreaded trips to the outhouse.

At this tender young age I had pretty much assembled my personal stable of heroes, not all of whom were the stuff of movies and comic books. High up on my list was James Harrison Butcher, my very own grandfather. He, too, was now another transplant to God's Country, once again at the whim of his nomadic daughter, my eccentric aunt. But for this I was grateful because I couldn't imagine life without him. Tall and stately at the age of eighty-two, he reluctantly relied upon a cane but still spent most of his days outdoors, chipping and chopping wood or hauling water from the well. I'd try to talk him into stopping to rest whenever I could, so I could cajole him into telling me yet another exciting tale about life in the olden days. There was nothing imaginary about *his* stories. He was born on May 2, 1868, the first male child in Bingham Canyon, Utah, after his family had crossed the country from Kentucky to Salt Lake City in prairie schooners. I learned that I evidently had an array of long-gone relatives who would easily fall into either of two categories: unsavory or wanted dead or alive. These were some of Brigham Young's accomplices who rode alongside him in his quest to populate the country with Mormons, phasing out those along the way who chose not to cooperate.

I'd settle at my grandfather's feet and anxiously wait for him to begin, watching him extract the tin of Prince Albert tobacco from his hip pocket and expertly fill the bowl of his pipe. One of his favorite anecdotes was when he was in that wrong place at that wrong time—a saloon—when a far-from-sober reveler got careless with his six-shooter, and an errant shot caught Grandpa in the shoulder. I closed my eyes and heard the barkeep shout, "That bullet has to come out—pronto!" Anesthesia of choice at the time was a generous shot of whiskey, a square of birch clamped between upper and lower dentures, and about twelve inches of water-soaked leather, half-inch width. The latter would be entwined around the patient's fingers, and the assistant surgeon would slowly twist and tighten the strip as the bullet was being dug out. This "medically induced distraction" was usually one hundred percent effective. The pitiful wailing emanating from the operating room was not the result of the ongoing surgery. And no matter how many times I heard the story, and knew that it ended well, I could not stop myself from jumping up and giving my Grandpa a big hug.

As for poor little Kathy, if the role I had cast her in that day was that of the fair maiden who was mercilessly abducted by enemies of the territory, she would wait patiently tied to a nearby tree, hoping Grandpa's story wouldn't take too long. She knew that in due time I would rescue her from the dastardly scoundrels who had spirited her away. I was her hero.

As for me, I can't remember how many times Grandpa had come to my rescue when some of my elaborate game plans went awry. On one occasion, when I had almost killed myself trying to jump onto my imaginary Stormy from the roof of the outhouse, he very skillfully told my mother that my skinned knees and elbows were the result of falling off the woodpile we were both working on. Grandpa assured me that it wasn't really a fib because that had actually happened one time, but just not that particular day. My hero.

One day I saw him storming from the outhouse, grumbling under his breath while he buckled his belt. "What's wrong?" I asked.

He didn't look up as he stomped past me. "My tobacco can fell out of my back pocket right down the damn toilet!"

The despair in his voice led me to surmise that this was the only tin of tobacco he owned, and projecting the consequences of this disaster even further, I considered the possibility that it could be the last remaining can of Prince Albert in the state of California. I sprang into action. Running into the house through the back door, I grabbed three wire coat hangers from the closet and raced out again. There was no time to waste. Hiding from sight behind the privy, I bent and twisted the hangers, looped them together and left an open hook at one end. Then I took a deep breath, stepped inside, and looked down. A faint glint of metal told me that Prince Albert had indeed plunged into the bowels of the ... well, into the bowels. I realized the task ahead of me was not going to be a pleasant one, and I might want to rethink it. But I knew there was no way I would change my mind. I was doing this for my Grandpa. My hero.

I gingerly lowered my invention into the abyss and tried to maneuver the wire around the tin. It was a two-fisted job, so I couldn't pinch my nose and had to resort to holding my breath, with intermittent pauses for gulps of air. After five or six attempts I was finally able to angle the hook onto the lip of the tin, and then very carefully inch it up the side wall until I could snatch it. I was not looking forward to that part, but getting out of there as quickly as possible had become a high priority. I threw the door open and flew down to the creek with my trophy. Fortunately, the lid had remained intact, so as I rinsed the tin I was pretty sure the tobacco was still in its pristine state. I was bursting with pride and couldn't wait to see my grandfather's face.

I returned to the house, the prize hidden behind my back. The family was chatting around the rickety kitchen table, while my grandfather sat on the edge of his bed that doubled as a sofa during the day. I slowly walked toward him, stopped, and then triumphantly presented Prince Albert. There was a moment of stunned silence as everyone's eyes locked onto the tin. They had obviously heard about his mishap because my mother looked like she was going to faint. My aunt was fixated on the apparatus dangling from my other hand, already mourning the loss of three perfectly good coat hangers. And my grandfather? Gingerly, he took the tin from me, turned it over a couple of times in the palm of his hand, but said nothing. I was now beginning to think that I had made a horrible mistake. He looked up and motioned me to come closer.

"C'mere," he said, gathering me to his chest in one of his crushing bear hugs. "You know what?" I shook my head, my bottom lip quivering. "You're my hero!"

Consider Disaster

ELIZABETH KIRKPATRICK-VRENIOS –
WRITERS OF THE MENDOCINO COAST

We considered our star, but never disaster,
the sputter and fizz of joy singular.
What did it matter what might not come after

the sauerkraut shine of a nuclear blaster
the space the tooth left, the kiss au revoir.
We considered our star, considered disaster

that tore open love's cloaks and left them in tatters.
Sharp bumblebee's sting, and wasp's repertoire
taught that it mattered what chatter came after.

Like the blindfold eye, the black-cloth shatter,
the tick's Lyme prick, the fall's chilly gnarr
we learned our star was meant for disaster,

as our inkling's nod faded faster
than the gas tank's last gasp, or unstrung guitar.
Nothing's the same the sickle leaves after

the trusted, rusted ball-peen hammer
has shattered and scattered our muddled memoir.
We consider our star, now hissing disaster
and yes! Oh yes, nothing comes after.

At the Far End of a Sturdy Branch

for Fran Claggett-Holland

STEVE TRENAM - REDWOOD WRITERS

You,
      who knew Robert Frost,
      and bought a Picasso
      with money you didn't have,
now greet me at your door
with a Saluki and a Whippet,
in a dress windswept
with charcoal brush strokes,
a necklace which only
your neck could honor,
and a smile to welcome me in.

The house brims with art.
A collusion of couches and chairs
brace themselves to accommodate
an entire tribe of poets.
The butcher block, scored
with decades of Madge's slices
in concert with flour from your hands.

As you speak of your two only sons,
both poets grown gray,
and Madge behind a permeable
membrane of memory—
I hear the music of
"the end of your beginning,
measuring out the days
grounded in rhythm and rhyme."

At one point I envision you
holding a cup of hot chocolate,
marshmallows melting on the surface,
afloat on the second movement
of Beethoven's *Pathétique*.

While you leave a lifetime
of astonished poets in your wake,
(every encounter a potential student)
I catch a glimpse of what
my life could have been,
and might still become.

High Frequency
J.D. BLAIR - MT. DIABLO

Randall Tims returned from the dentist with several new fillings, and that night as he lay in bed in the quiet of a clear November night, his teeth began receiving radio broadcasts. He believed that the music was coming from the neighbor girl who kept her windows open and had her radio too loud when in fact what he heard was coming from his left molar. He turned over and went to sleep to Classic Rock 105. The next night when Randall went to bed, he slept easily at first, but after a few hours, woke with Brahms' Symphony No. 2 ringing in his ears. His right bicuspid was picking up a broadcast out of Salt Lake City. Randall tossed and turned until he finally dropped off to sleep listening to Starlight Symphonies from KQEL.

Over several weeks Randall's mouth picked up programming from a wide range of formats: everything from rock to classical and oldies, folk, and talk. One night his first bicuspid engaged in a heated exchange with a wisdom tooth over the merits of back-channel diplomacy in the Middle East. He slept little that night, frustrated that he couldn't take part in the discussion. On another night he tossed and turned when a pirate radio station off the coast of Mexico played every top ten rock and roll oldie between 1956 and 1965. Randall claimed that a lateral incisor and a cuspid were actually vibrating during the entire musical countdown.

When Randall went in for his next dental checkup, he told his dentist that his mouth was picking up radio signals and the dentist said Randall was probably hallucinating.

"You would have to have a very large antenna to pick up such a wide range of programming," said the dentist.

The dentist told Randall to try rearranging the furniture in his bedroom which he did, but that only increased the volume of the broadcasts that now included satellite programming. Tims was getting shock jocks ranting in his ear at all hours of the night, commercial free.

Randall returned to the dentist who replaced the fillings, reduced the amount of metal in the amalgam, and sent Randall on his way. He slept well for a few weeks until the night he started picking up strange, coded messages bombarding his wisdom teeth. He was listening in on top-secret exchanges between Washington and the United Arab Emirates.

"Helium balloons stretched thin above arid oases," said the UAE.

"Knicks 94, Raptors 88," answered Washington.

For an entire month Tims was barraged with ciphers from every corner of the world.

"Winter in Norway is balmy," sent NATO headquarters.

"Klaatu Verada Nikto," responded Area 51.

When his wisdom teeth weren't picking up ciphers, his lower bicuspids were taking shout-outs from truckers on the interstate.

"This is Big Dog from Denver, c'mon back."

"Big Dog, this is Top Gun on a heading out of Tucson, what are you hauling? C'mon back."

"Spuds from Idaho," responded Big Dog.

Top Gun was carrying a load of farm workers out of Arizona.

One night an upper bicuspid began beeping when it received an SOS call from a thirty-foot sloop in trouble off the coast of Newfoundland. The boat was sending out an alert signal that was being boosted by the boat's mast. Randall called the Coast Guard who located the boat, towed it to safety, and rescued the two people on board.

After several months Randall got into a routine of listening to his teeth each night and discovered that by positioning his jaw just right on the pillow and moving his teeth in certain ways, he could surf the airwaves and change stations. He became adept at listening for announcements of the time allowing him to wake himself each morning without an alarm clock.

Randall became accustomed to his mouth's receptions but soon was frustrated that it wasn't enough. He wanted broadband so on his next checkup instructed the dentist to give him a full set of braces. The dentist balked saying it wasn't necessary, but Randall insisted, and the dentist complied. Today Randall's mouth is capable of picking up audio signals from both radio and television worldwide, and he's working on a technique that will allow him to listen in stereo.

Lunar Eclipse #1

PAMELA HECK - REDWOOD WRITERS

Boldly she presents herself,
full moon
on a rain flecked night,
unperturbed as shadow
strokes her face
and then devours
each shining morsel,
bit by bit.

The shadow of a world
glides by with swift precision.
It lacks the tenacity
of one dark thought
that lingers.

The Hummingbird's Flight

HEATHER FURNAS - REDWOOD WRITERS

Nesting in my father's
boyish hand,
woodchips flying,
tempera brush dancing,
the bird hatched,
all rose-stem green
leashed in cardinal,
and given to his aunt.

Her gift hung on the wall
as its creator grew up,
wars started,
wars ended,
her husband died,
I was born,
then my children,
and she grew old.

In her eighties,
she gave me the bird,
now an heirloom
for me to pass on,
her gesture protecting it
from the Oakland Fire
that took her home
and all but her nightgown.

From my own wall,
the hummingbird
finally took flight
in a wildfire,
its ashes swirling,
leaving only memories
like a watercolor
drowning in rain.

Yesterday I looked
outside at a hummingbird
floating in air
as I called my father
and answered the same
question over and over
until I said I loved him,

In Progress

ARLEEN EAGLING - TRI-VALLEY WRITERS

December was less than a week away. Another year sliding down the drain, and another office job about to end with a thud.

I'd begged my friend Petra to come over that night. She paused in the doorway of my tiny kitchen. I could never imagine myself looking as sharp as she did, even at 3 a.m. She'd dressed all in black except for her shimmering white scarf. The only black I had was my straggly hair. My shapeless gray sweats matched how I felt.

"You seem worn down, Melanie," she said. "Have you slept at all?"

"Last night, maybe about four hours," I said. "Guess it's time for more coffee. I wish I had your energy without gulping caffeine." I'd never seen her tired.

I pointed to the clunky chair I kept for guests at my table for two. That wooden furniture had been the single useful part of my childhood I held onto.

"Petra, I didn't want to do this to you again, but I pleaded for a chance to work on this special project. It's for the December issue, and now they tell me to rework it."

My hands shook as I stood at the stove to pour my coffee. I moaned. "Why can't I even get this right? Every morning I do it in a fog."

She didn't respond, probably impatient already.

"But this is not every morning," I said quickly. "I promise, no more complaints. And don't worry that I'll be distracted tonight. My phone battery just died."

Petra was unpredictable, and I knew better than to annoy her. We'd been friends since I moved to Hayes Street, near the Haight, a couple years after I gave up on college. One afternoon I sat at Starbucks, plodding through revisions to a ghost story, and she simply sat down at my table. We talked for a good two hours. The first time she came to my apartment, she showed up long after midnight. She'd been visiting a friend and saw lights at my window.

This time, I'd dragged my floor lamp into the kitchen and put a bottle of water ready for her on the table. I forgot about the granola crumbs with my PC and cell phone on the placemat. Petra stacked it all neatly on a counter behind her before she sat.

"Nice phone, Mel," she said, pointing at its shiny, zebra-striped case.

I brought over my sugary coffee and sat on the folding chair beside her. "I wanted to upgrade it this year, but phones were too expensive. I bought a case instead. If I get promoted, rather than fired, I'll buy a new cell."

"Sounds smart." She politely folded her hands on the table. "Mel, here's a big question for you: Why do you assume I can help you? I'm flattered that you trust me, but why?"

I bit my lip. She'd never asked such a thing before. I thought she understood me.

"Right now? Petra, I'll grab any chance you could make things better. Seeing you has always helped me."

She didn't respond. My hands went cold. I remembered a time we disagreed about one of the ancient Greek myths. When I left the room to grab a reference book, she disappeared.

"Are you going to stop coming?" I asked, my mind faltering. "Am I too greedy for your time? My Queen Cleo-Petra?" I reached for her hand but she moved it to her lap.

"Relax, you're fine. Don't answer my question right away, but you ought to think about what we're doing." She pulled something from her pocket. "Look at this little thing I found. See what you can do with it."

I had to laugh. She handed me a turtle-shaped candle about three inches long. It had a wild mix of bright spots on the shell, four stubby feet, and a tiny head. Its face showed no emotion, not even a pretend smile to make it cute.

"He appears to be a rather uninspired turtle, aside from his shell," I said, putting it down.

A slight softening of features was Petra's version of a smile. She positioned the turtle between us at the corner of the table, as if he peered over the edge, then pressed a finger on his back so he wouldn't fall. Her solemn expression returned.

"Does he feel motivated yet?"

"Oh, definitely!" I said. "He's quivering with fear. There's a torrential storm and gobs of mud down the slope ahead. He realizes he's someplace he shouldn't be."

Petra abruptly lifted her finger. I caught the turtle before he fell and put him farther from the ledge, facing the opposite way.

"He changes direction," I said. On impulse, I set my coffee mug a couple inches from his nose. "But that storm washed the trail out. Now there's a huge obstruction in front of him."

"Is he doomed?" she asked.

"Well, some old myth or other warned him a journey would involve obstacles. Maybe he will prevail. The boulder might crack and crumble. Or a landslide could move it away."

"Not good enough, Melanie. Those are acts of God, not the turtle. Is he or is he not our focus here?"

I sighed. "You're right. It's about the turtle."

I stared at our hero and the imposing ceramic mug blocking his way. I pictured him bracing himself, pushing against the thick handle, unable to move it. I felt his desperation. Then I remembered: turtles aren't only about determination. They also have strong legs.

"So, he'll dig under and around the block of stone and continue on his path," I announced. "Okay! I'm getting looser, Petra. Another cup of coffee might do it."

I got up, preoccupied with turtle thoughts, although keeping an eye on her. She shifted slightly in her seat. Was she bored? I needed all of her attention. To keep her focus on me, I stirred my coffee, clanking the spoon. I pulled out my chair with a thump before I sat down.

"Let's try a different idea," she said. "What if you could give up your day job and be okay financially, writing what you really love? I mean, doing work that won't upset your family or ruin your credit score. In fact, it would cost nothing at all. Like a fantasy come true."

I sipped my coffee, thinking along with her. It seemed ideal, so far.

"A cost must be there somewhere. Nothing meaningful comes from nothing."

"Sure, risks are involved. You'd still depend on other people for marketing and all that, so there's the usual problem you have with teamwork. Or, you might talk yourself into failing."

"Now you sound like a job counselor. You could almost be a literary agent."

She leaned back in her chair. "No, my friend. I would not aspire to that."

Major mistake. I totally changed her mood, praising her for talent she took no pride in.

"Listen, Petra, I didn't mean it's what you *should* be. I meant you're good with people. At my job, being an unskilled backup gofer for the boss, people act like I'm their servant. Maybe my miserable childhood and some bad choices got me where I am. But I'm nearly thirty years old and barely have the self-control to collaborate."

I knew that serious character flaw of mine, the colossal boulder I had to push and scratch my way around. No acts of God; only my efforts could correct it.

Petra scowled. "I know. You haven't quite learned to accommodate help from other people. You keep yourself too closed up."

"But I keep asking for your suggestions. You are gifted, how you figure people out."

"Some of them," she said. For a moment she stared past me, across the room. "I do love that you listen, though. A person like you, with your potential.... But I'm flying blind, Mel. You haven't let me see what you're working on."

"Right. When I do lousy work, I don't want anyone to see it. I already know it's junk." I glanced away from her, uncomfortable. "My piece is completely flat."

She crossed her arms over her chest, her voice suddenly harsh. "So, what do you want me here for, exactly? Are we supposed to just sit and cry over this?"

"No, no! You keep me thinking straight! This is my first real opportunity to write. My boss said it better shine, or forget about a promotion. Meaning, forget about my job."

I rubbed my forehead, hoping my explanation would make sense.

"Petra? This time, it isn't fiction. It's a profile piece about a poet who gave a reading at my school, years ago. Her early life was incredibly rough, yet she didn't give up. She learned how to move beyond her misery. And her work is amazing."

"So, that's what has you stuck? All right, give me a second to concentrate." She closed her eyes briefly. I bit my lip hard.

"Follow me now, Melanie. First, take a deep breath and slowly let it out." She paused, so I obeyed. "Now, recall an interesting town you visited, or maybe a song you've loved since high school, or a marvelous smell which forever reminds you of Christmas. Remember how the situation made you happy and hopeful. Approach that mental place. Absorb it into your body." Her voice drifted, gentle once again.

My eyes closed and I allowed my mind to wander into a peaceful state. I settled on the memory of an expensive but beautiful bakery cake, more perfect than any you'd bake at home.

"It's the cake for my tenth birthday," I said.

"Tell me about it."

"For my birthday party, I'd asked for a special cake with ten roses surrounding my name. The cake smelled wonderful, like friendship and joy." I sighed, remembering. "For my party, my mother even sewed us matching dresses with a red rose print.

That year I'd made new friends and desperately wanted to believe I was growing up."

I kept my eyes closed, imagining Petra would be pleased. I waited, listening to the ticking clock on my kitchen wall and the refrigerator rumbling softly in a corner. I heard Petra scuff her chair on the linoleum floor. The tone of her voice changed.

"Now," she said, "imagine a disturbance which could interfere with your vision. Let the disruption intrude upon your memory. Let it come. Risk a real tragedy. Go where it takes you."

I sensed something else take over. I opened my eyes and there stood a domineering woman, dressed in black, hands on her hips. She had the same ferocious expression my mother had when she got drunk. My heart beat faster. I forced my thoughts back to events I had tried for years to forget. I spoke about what happened, holding the poison of it as far away as I could.

"At first, during the party, my mother was cheerful and charming. Then she heard an older girl say my cake looked like a wedding cake that went flat. I can hear echoes of my mother shouting terrible things. I see her face at the moment she abruptly shoved my cake off the table in front of my horrified friends. I remember every one of them immediately left to go home."

Years later, sitting in my kitchen, I could feel the searing humiliation of that day. Petra must have known I could, and still she kept after me.

"Dig deeper, Mel," she demanded. "You're not done."

I went on, my hands clenched into fists.

"My mother's drinking ruined everything. My cake, smashed on the floor. My friends, afraid of her. I could not undo any part of the catastrophe. I was so mortified that I...."

There I stopped. I'd finally talked about that disaster. That should have been enough.

Petra pushed for more. "You did what, Mel? You need to say it."

"No! I've never told this to anyone. Why should I now?"

Her reply caught me off guard.

"Because you want to," she said.

That wasn't true, but it also was. Both of us knew it. In the midst of all my drama, I realized she had an honest concern for me. I did want her to understand. I answered slowly, staring at the floor.

"You ask what else I did. I made a frantic plan to run away that same night." I looked up at her. "But my mom and I, we only had each other. I couldn't leave her. I didn't know how to get help for either of us. So, that's all. I just stayed."

My buried memories of shock and defeat had been dragged into the light. I felt dizzy. And angry. Did Petra think the pain I'd released into the room would conveniently fade away? It did not. I got up, standing near enough to slap her, although I didn't. She stepped back from me. I leaned closer and kept my voice low.

"Now you know the most shameful experience of my life. Are you satisfied?"

She seemed puzzled. "Melanie, I am happy you persevered with this. I only wanted you to see what's been in your way."

"My life is complicated. If you expect psychological games to solve everything, guess again. And yet I did realize something tonight: I can refuse to allow myself another failure."

I stood upright, feeling energy throughout my body for the first time in days.

"I am writing about someone I admire. I don't need any creaky old hero myth to frame it. I'll scrape aside my gritty messes and create a vision of the poet that glows from within her life. I'll use the tenacity I know is in me. My miserable past is, at long last, worth something to me."

I had no more to say. Petra remained silent, her arms hanging limp.

"You should go now," I said.

She nodded, walked from the room, and was gone.

I replaced my turtle candle on a shelf in the front room. I refilled my mug to begin a new session on the laptop. I had work to do. My article would contain every component needed to make the editor proud. It would illuminate a marvelous poet and the strong commitment she made to her chosen life. And a clarity I owed to Petra would shine through.

Seated at the table, calm once again, I made a promise to myself. Next time–if there would be a next time–I'd make sure to offer her my thanks before we started. She deserved that. About to recharge my phone, I picked it up and, somehow, a new text arrived.

It said, "You're welcome."

I laughed. As I said, Petra was good with people.

threshold
a pantoum in practice

SKYE BLAINE - REDWOOD WRITERS

window door or gate
entrance to another place
a change a shift—fresh start
clean breath new step

entrance to another place
look down, the doorsill beckons
clean breath new step
begin again again and yet again

look down, the doorsill beckons
breath will cleanse your heart
begin again again and yet again
a new threshold awaits

breath will cleanse your heart
open wide and trust
a new threshold awaits
be brave and take that step

window door or gate
a change a shift—fresh start

A Walk Before the Storm

JEN SCHOEN - REDWOOD WRITERS

As the plague spreads
I walk a trail
along the laguna
drinking in the beauty
of my West County home

The pond
wears a blanket
of velvet-red algae
Wild mustard
glows gold
among the vines

The sky shimmers
in iridescent blue
stretching from the hulk
of Mount Saint Helena
to the forested hills
of the Russian River

Clusters of cumulus
form a menagerie
snow-white lambs
cavort with cotton ball bunnies
while gray-wooly mammoths
form a silent
stampede

Over my head
the clouds turn to silver
with inky-blue edges
still sunshine
warms my face

Black clusters form
on the horizon as
thunder threatens
from behind

Planet Earth
feels poised
on a precipice
suspended
in the moment
before a deluge

Invisible Songs

MARA LYNN JOHNSTONE - REDWOOD WRITERS

A year ago, my world went silent. The doctors told me the particulars, which of several genetic disorders was to blame, but I had enough shouting elders in my family that it wasn't a surprise. Heartbreaking, yes; surprising, no. Twelve months since I've heard a human voice, and I only spent one in rage and despair.

That first month was a wash of tears. I deleted every MP3 I'd ever owned, and snapped all my CDs but a treasured few. Cranked the volume of the TV up to max until I felt the floor shake and saw a neighbor's shadow at the door. They probably knocked, but how would I know? I turned the volume down, and the shadow went away.

Eventually the depression ebbed into resignation. I had seen this from the outside; now it was my turn. Family had shown me what to expect.

But nobody said anything about the music.

Eleven months ago, I heard a soaring aria, faint and tinny but real. I stood up in my living room, rotating in place, trying to find the source. A silhouette passing the window told me that someone had probably rung the doorbell. But my doorbell didn't sound like that.

I yanked open the door in time to see a delivery person heading back to her truck. She gave me a wave, her steps jaunty, and her attention elsewhere. I was too dumbstruck to wave back. As

2022 LITERARY REVIEW 73

she got into the truck and zoomed away, the music faded. I stepped forward to follow, and stumbled against a package.

Everything was quiet again. The package was nothing: some light bulbs and soap I'd ordered online. My thoughts whirling, I took it inside and spent a frustrating afternoon trying to find things that I could hear.

Since I worked from home, sending many an email about web development and rarely seeing people face-to-face, it was a while before I heard the music again. This time I had gone out to empty the trash, and as I lowered the lid with its usual silence, a burst of death metal made me jump.

No one was behind me with speakers, or in a nearby yard having a party. The only person on the street was the neighbor across the way, who was scraping his shoe on the grass with dramatic fury.

I stared. He was clearly shouting, waving his arms and everything, but all I heard was discordant electric guitars.

A child appeared at his window, surely asking what had happened, and the tempo slowed. By the time the man had left his shoes by the door and gone inside, the tune in my ears sounded more like classic rock. It wasn't a song I'd ever heard before.

I left the trash can and circled the block, listening as hard as I could. With each neighbor I encountered, their voices were silent, but something sang.

The woman gardening sounded like a pastoral scene in a movie, all skirling flutes and good cheer. The man carrying groceries from his car sounded like a workout montage as he strained to lift all the bags at once. The children playing soccer each had a different version of the same song following them about. It spiked with excitement when someone scored a goal, and hummed in anticipation when the next round began.

I didn't know what to make of this. It was exciting, baffling, alarming. I went home and scheduled a doctor's appointment. That was eleven months ago. By then the doctor had tested everything and said politely that he didn't believe me. I gave up on answers with some bitterness.

Nine months ago, I started spending time in coffee shops for the music. Many people passed through, some staying longer than others. At first it was exhilarating, being able to hear something, many somethings! But the songs were unpleasant more often than not, accompanying people under stress of one type or another. I tried other places where people gathered: the park, the movie theater, even the library. That one was the most likely to sound peaceful, but not as much as I'd expected. I started to get discouraged.

Eight months ago, I heard a crow sing.

It was so unlike the rough caw that I remembered, I stopped in my tracks and laughed. The crow was happily eating something: a bit of fast food that someone had left on a bench, and the music surrounding it was the most cheerful of reggae tunes. When I laughed, it startled and flew off in a flutter of chase-scene drums. I apologized to it and crossed the street so it could return to such a delightful meal. Instead of going home, I went to the woods outside of town for some birdwatching with a smile on my face.

Seven months ago, I did my research, cleared space in the yard, bought the supplies, and built a proper atrium. I filled it with the happiest songbirds you've ever heard. They have their every need met, and I spend a good portion of my days there, laptop at hand and seeds ready to scatter. I can't hear the chirps of my birds, or the jingle of their playthings, but I hear their joy.

Web development pays well, thankfully, and I haven't lacked in funds to care for my new feathered family. They are happy, and I thought seven months ago that I'd heard the best there was to hear.

Then six months ago, a cat passed through my yard, and sang me a new song. One of curiosity, and stealth, and a mix of peace and excitement that the birds could never match.

I started researching again.

Five months ago, I brought home three adult cats that the shelter knew to be sisters. The car ride was full of anxious violins, but once they explored the house and realized they could stay, they sang me a song full of such purring love that I couldn't stop crying.

By the four month mark, they had settled into a routine of sunbeams, treats, windows overlooking the atrium, and the occasional high-octane gallop through the house. My life is no longer silent. It is full of an ever-changing orchestra of largely good moods.

Three months ago, I set up a "catio" on the other side of the yard from the atrium, to let the cats spend time out in the breeze without worrying about losing them to cars or dogs. They like this arrangement just fine, and the birds have learned to ignore them.

Two months ago, I was sure that this time, I was set.

One month ago, I was even more certain.

Yesterday I took a walk by the river, and heard a fish sing. It was devastatingly beautiful.

Today I am researching aquariums.

Cowgirl

EDWINA ROMERO - LONG BEACH

I sold that big hoss ya' wanted, she says without guilt.
He'da made a fine English hoss, tho.
Sold 'im last week for six hunnerd.

She knows the importance of jeans and strong leather gloves,
muck boots, and grey Stetson hats.
Has no patience for fringed mini-skirts, silky red shirts, faux
   cowhide vests.

Remember that there th'roughbred? she says. And
I recall sharp flanks, molting chestnut, apathetic eyes.
Been starved, she'd said. Stock's the first to go.
I'll fatten 'im up. If you don't want 'im.

She smiles and the space where a tooth used to be is not
   embarrassed.
She wears no tethers, shows no teats, her mane falls western
   style
unclipped, unpulled, unbraided.
She laughs and coughs, spits if she needs to.

Sold 'im for six hunnerd.
He'da made a fine jumper tho'. Too big for packin'.
Can't get them heavy packs up there.
I don't ask about ladders or mounting blocks.

Can't pack them heavy ladders now, canya'? she says.
She cackles, coughs, and spits. Lands one at the side of
  my foot.
Six hunnerd, she says as she walks away,
and the dust cloud reaches my nose.

Readers are Still Waiting

After Lawrence Ferlinghetti, 1919-2021
MARY LANGER THOMPSON - HIGH DESERT

We wait for the multitudes on Mulberry Street
to be lifted up in all their diversity,
for The Borrowers to stop stealing and calling it borrowing,
and for one velveteen rabbit to get fluffed up again.

We wait for Nancy Drew to solve mysteries of life
and Meg and Charles to iron out those wrinkles in time,
for Archie to choose between Betty and Veronica,
and for the Hardy Boys to become hardier in a Brave New World.

We still hope for the killing of mockingbirds to stop,
for human comedy laughter,
and for Vonnegut's Dresden to push the bombs back into the sky
before they incinerate people. So it goes.

And I am still waiting for Maya to continue
to free those singing caged birds,
for Mango Street to be safe for Esperanza,
and, like Langston and Lawrence, for America to be America again.

Land of Goodness and Hope

KAREN SUNDBACK - SAN FRANCISCO PENINSULA

I wake befuddled to a desolation I've never known. It's as if God's hand had pulled my hometown's skyscrapers out of the ground by their roots, sucked the Pacific Ocean dry, and flattened its characteristic hills like boxes ready for recycling. After that, God sprinkled the Earth with cacti, scrub, sand, and rocks. Before me lies a barren land stretching for unimaginable distances, testing the limits of my vision. It's so dry that pebbles crackle underfoot, breaking the absolute silence of a dead land. No birds sing or insects fill the sky. No life at all.

This is not San Francisco. How did I get here? How long have I been here? The pain in my head, I've felt it before. It's from gamma hydroxybutyric acid. Damn you, Joe! He slipped me a Mind Eraser again. But why? I check my pocket for my cell phone—gone. Even the cheap Timex, a present for my eleventh birthday, is missing from my wrist. I have nothing in this wilderness but my clothes.

Why would Joe, my dependable drug dealer, leave me here? My head aches thinking about it. He's always said I was his best customer and wanted the best for me and my career at Big Bucks. He kept me on the lowest dose of amphetamines so that my work was top notch. He likened me to an athlete in training for the Olympics. Antidepressants only during crises. Ambien when I was desperate for sleep. All reasonable, right?

But then Joe had a mischievous side, like the time when he offered me a free sample of a new "healthy" pill. It happened not long ago during our regular Saturday morning brunch—a very civilized manner for scoring drugs, don't you think? He raved about the pill—what steroids did for muscles is what this pill could do for my cognitive abilities. Only he lied. The pill was gamma hydroxybutyric acid—the Mind Eraser. It turned me into a zombie—walking, talking, and remembering nothing.

Apparently feeding me the Mind Eraser gave Joe the vacation he so badly deserved. He drove my car, sat me in the passenger seat, and we traveled to places he always wanted to go. And best of all, even in my "living-dead" state, I could conveniently sign for the hotel and meal bills. Greatest time ever for Joe!

Not so much for me. No more "healthy" pills for me! I stuck with my old dependable friends after that. And of course, Joe apologized. So, everything's fine, right?

During my zombie week Joe didn't rummage through my condo, did he? Didn't see that I sold my condo for a down payment for a new house? The funds from the sale will be in my bank account this week. I can't believe that Joe would abandon me here to empty my bank account. Can you?

Why am I joking about this? The truth is I'm frightened. The indescribable loneliness is terrifying. When I was a child, I'd bury my head in Aunt Louise's lap after a fight with a friend or when someone else got better grades. She'd hold me and talk with me until I calmed down. Everything seemed better with her.

What did she teach us Camp Fire Girls about survival skills ten years ago when I was thirteen? *If you know the general direction to safety, find a distant landmark to guide you there in case you lose the trail.* Of course! If Joe drove me out here, there would be tire marks around here somewhere. Let's see.

Aha! Here they are! The truck's scar across the scrubland will eventually lead me to a road—and to help. I set my eyes on the northern skyline above the scar, fixing each outcrop and crenulation in my mind's eye.

Find water and shelter. According to the sun, I've been walking for less than an hour when the track leads me to a prickly pear cactus. Water! I set to work preparing the pads. But—surprise! Visions of Joe loom in that poor cactus and I pounce on it with the ferocity of a mob during Black Friday. I savagely kick off the pads, then the spines off the pads. Done with that, I finish my assault by picturing Joe's face on the rocky desert floor and "bloody" his face by jabbing his image repeatedly with red prickly pear fruit. It's difficult work; I'm sweating, but in the end it feels good. My well justified fury now vented, I settle down to my task, fastening the pads together like pearls on a necklace using the laces from my Merrill boots. Ta-da! A headdress to shade me from the sun. The Camp Fire Girls would have giggled with glee at my contraption, but Aunt Louise would have been pleased. The fibrous pad is as appealing as green Styrofoam, but the juice is divine. Chewing on my prize I set out again, trudging along the truck's path.

My feet hurt. I've been walking for miles and miles, farther than I've ever walked in my life. Following me is a shrub with greenish white leaves. It dots the land, so no matter how far I travel, it's always here. Curious, I crush one of the leaves and sniff it—sage, Aunt Louise's favorite. Whenever I needed comfort, she would hold me close. Before I left for Berkeley, she held me so tightly. I towered over her and buried my nose in her thin white hair. The crushed leaf in my hand smells of her. Breaking off a sprig, I sniff it, put it in my pocket, and press on.

The morning's still cool, the air fresh. I'm getting the better of this desert—I'm sure—until I stop dead. The trail up ahead has disappeared! The tire tracks are my only chance out of here. Without them, this place's a deathtrap. I yell in frustration until I'm hoarse . . . and calm. Taking a deep breath, I turn over the situation in my mind. Looking back, I can't tell how far I've come. The desert behind and all around looks the same, only this exposed rock looks different. Ahead to the right is rocky bumpy scrubland, to the left is smooth fast bedrock, into which the tire tracks disappear. I put myself in Joe's shoes: Which is the quickest way to dispose of a body (namely, mine)? The sandstone highway to the left, of course!

I reach a northern ridge and stand under a blistering sun. The air sears my lungs. I'm not sweating, so I tear into another pad from my headdress to suck out the precious liquid. The shadow at my feet, which has slanted left all morning, at that moment slants right.

Until now I hadn't realized how lucky I was—Joe's Mind Eraser had numbed my body and mind, so I didn't feel the cruelest elements: heat, thirst, drug withdrawal. Being a walking, half-witted zombie in this wasteland was a blessing. But it's over. The effects of his potion—which felt like Novocain shot into my brain—is wearing off, and my mind clears. Damn you, Joe! Ghosts of amphetamines and antidepressants tug at each of my nerves—seven trillion neurons clamor for one more pill. A pill or two, it's not much to ask to quiet my jangled nerves or soothe my aching body, is it? With just a pill or two, my stomach would unclench, and I wouldn't shake. I won't be a mess, I'd be alright. I've tried life without my little friends; it didn't work. I want them back.

Remember girls! Never panic. All you need to do is to put one foot in front of the other. It's that simple! I sigh heavily. As far as my eyes can see, everything's dead—rocks, sand, even the bushes hide their vitality deep in the bowels of the earth, safe from this deadly sun. The view of the valley is like looking into amber resin and finding life fossilized, captured for the ages. I make a bet with myself: If any form of life shows itself before I finish singing "American Anthem," then I'll think of a reason for giving up drugs. So, I stand upon that high point and hum the tune and pick out a few remembered words. "...America, America I gave my best to you..." I gave my best, but to whom? Not to her who devoted her life to me. I'm so sorry, Aunt Louise.

No movement during the entire song. Resigned, I search for my friendly crenulated landmark. Which way to go?

But then—movement on the other side of the vast bowl of the arroyo, so far away I can barely detect it. It might be a tumbleweed cartwheeling under the western peaks, only there's not a whisper of wind. It's a vehicle! Moving slowly across the valley floor, so distant and small, it could be an ant's car.

I found the road. It seems an impossible distance, but there's prickly pear along the way to keep me alive. Now all I need is a clear path to the road. Before I set off again, for good luck, I pronounce my reason for quitting drugs—this place. If I ever get out, I won't let drugs bring me back here or anyplace like this again.

The day's dying, the sun sinks wearily towards the mountains. Within hours nightfall comes. Parts of the lonely desert highway peek in and out of sight. Exhaustion is my only companion, and it lends no words of encouragement. Only Aunt Louise's memory cheers me: *Remember girls, the most important thing about surviving the wilderness is hope.* Aunt Louise with her Buzz

Lightyear attitude of "To Infinity and Beyond!" and her latest Macy's fashions. She would wear capri pants to show off her most outrageous stockings, as we romped in the woods, as if survival would be child's play. But even my aunt's most encouraging memories fail me as enervation elbows its way back to exact its toll.

Cool air comes just in the nick of time.

I sing Schubert's "Ave Maria" and find a bright side to my isolation: No one complains about my singing. The words evoke memories of a soprano whose seraphic voice transcends anything on Earth and who soothes the cactus balls in my belly and the pounding in my head. " . . . 'Tis thou, 'tis thou canst save me amid despair . . ."

To the west, the dying sun catches the glint of a pair of lights, so small they could be reflections in the eye of a lizard waking to the evening chill. But the lights grow steadily brighter. Are those red and blue lights mounted on its roof? I run as fast as my shaky legs can take me—and keep running until my lungs wheeze.

But wait just a minute. Let me catch my breath and marvel at my good fortune. Soon I'll have drugs and my SF life again, free of pain and this terrible weariness. I want it so badly; I'd do anything for it.

But what about Aunt Louise? I miss her so.

Yet I can't have both. She can never know about the drugs.

The vehicle's close enough to see it's a patrol car. If I don't move soon, it will drive past.

Girls! When help arrives, don't hesitate! Save yourselves because you may get only one chance. Don't let your friends and family down. Think of all they've done for you! Aunt Louise has always been there for me. When I left home, every day she texted me throughout my time at Berkeley and Big Bucks—and

I never had time to talk with her, unless I needed something. I've treated her so badly, and yet she would be devastated if I never returned. No matter how much I put her off, she cares for me.

I care for her so much that I run as fast as my wobbly legs can carry me—to the road.

Summer Heaven

ANNE MARIE WENZEL - SAN FRANCISCO PENINSULA

The rhythmic synchronism of the crickets enthralls me,
reminds me
of summers long ago, of a life impassioned.

Rubbing their forewings together, the night chorists draw
me outside
where a lone guitarist cries another love song through a window.

How do I make this beauty plain to you? Perhaps I'll take
your shoulders
and push you into the night surrounded by stars,

or drive you to the desert where there'll be a rainstorm
and together
we'll inhale the essence of the wet desert sage, because

if you never experience the cricket song on a cool August night
or never
smell the Nevada desert after a rain, how will you know?

If you never clamber over boulders alongside a rushing creek
or never
sight an eagle soaring over open country, how will you know?

If you never thrill to the sound of the wind in the trees
or never
count the many greens of a mossy rainforest, how will you know?

If you never pause for the dance of tree shadows on the wall
or never
feel a song rise from your fingertips to your soul

how will you know,

how will you know,

how will you know me?

The Artist and the Huntress

SANDY MOFFETT - WRITERS OF KERN

We both hear it
the buzz of wings
as the tiny torpedo hovers near the window.

We both see it
the flash of color
from this feathered prism.

We both gaze on it
the artist, pen in hand
unable to document the true beauty.

The other
the huntress, tail flicking
only a glass barrier saves her intended prey.

Lessons by the Sea

LIZ ABESS - SACRAMENTO

The cold, ominous day warned me not to swim. Waves crashed on shore with angry force in response to the churning ocean. Yet, even then, the Santa Cruz ocean beckoned me with its clashing peace and power. As I neared the water's edge the salty smell and spray of the surf seduced me like a forbidden kiss.

My best friend, Susan, and I spent two weeks every summer on the beach, our annual playground. I was eleven when we found ourselves—newly declared blood sisters—with her parents and our brothers in a lonely line of townhouses on La Selva Beach. Most days I savored the sunshine warming my head, the sand crunching between my toes, and the water dripping off my twiggy frame.

But on Wednesday the marine layer of fog refused to burn off. We skipped barefoot down to the water's edge and dodged a few waves before deciding the chill made the blackened Pacific less alluring. Our older and wiser brothers rented wetsuits for the day. When they finished swimming, Susan and I asked if we could borrow them.

Down on the bottom deck we slid into those oversized suits like knights donning their shining armor, thrilled we'd be swimming despite the sub-fifty-degree outside temperature. We didn't mind the loose fit; we cuffed the rubbery black neoprene at our wrists and ankles until our hands and feet were exposed.

Once armed against the cold, we traipsed across the white sand from her parents' rented unit, five hundred yards to the sea. I spotted no other die-hard swimmers around to witness our swagger; her parents read books and drank cocktails on the third-floor deck. A couple—in zipped jackets and cuffed pants—walked their dog in the distance.

We skipped through the foamy surf where it met the sand and jumped beyond the baby waves. Once deep enough, I dove into the roaring water, safe inside in my wetsuit. Susan followed. I paddled to the ideal depth and turned around, hoping to catch one of the breakers for a bodysurf ride. I passed on more waves than I rode in the charged sea, well acquainted with the waves' power. If I mistimed a wave it would smash me into the hard ocean floor.

My elation diminished fifteen minutes later when I noticed cold water inside my wetsuit. Though I continued treading at the break point, my buoyance was sinking along with my heart. *Why wasn't I able to ride more waves?*

"Hey, do you have water in your suit?" I asked, swimming closer to Susan. "I think it's coming through the neck part and weighing me down."

"Yea, mine, too," said Susan still eight feet away.

"We should probably go in," I said. Fear glazed my thoughts like lip balm, hardly noticeable.

"Yeah, let's go." I heard her teeth-chattering voice and felt colder.

The sky grew darker as we inched toward shore. I couldn't touch the ground yet, so my typical dancer's leaps were out of the question. The shoreline summoned, only forty feet away. Despite our reputation as little fish, I recognized after a few minutes we weren't getting closer.

I glanced at Susan and sensed her struggling. *Why was this taking so long?* I kept swimming diagonally, trying to generate security by shrinking the side-by-side space between us and the land.

"I feel like I'm not going anywhere," I said, four feet from Susan.

"Me neither. Is it the wetsuits? We've never had trouble before!"

"I don't know. Paddle harder." I ordered us both. I was seven months older; she was more athletic.

I cupped my hands and pulled at the menacing seawater in a sloppy breaststroke, legs frog-kicking behind. Land teased thirty feet away, close, but not reachable. Water in my wetsuit swelled around my ankles as I fought against the retreating waves.

"I'm not sure I can do this," I said, breathing faster. *Did I have the strength to make it to shore?*

"We have to keep swimming." Susan gasped out the words between strokes. I recognized distress in her high-pitched mandate. *Was she trying to convince me or herself?* She'd always led me in our childhood adventures, whether jumping off my garage roof like Mary Poppins or sneaking out at night with the neighborhood kid across the street.

"I'm. Kinda. Scared." I said between breaths, scouring the beach for a rescuer.

I spied her parents standing, staring from the deck, a sandy football field away, books and cocktails down, leaning with hands on the deck rail, fully dressed in jeans and sweatshirts. Their body language spoke concern, but they were too far away to know our danger level—our heads were still above water. They'd never reach us in time if we sank. I scanned the shore and saw no one else.

As I continued to paddle in, the water tugged me out, folding me like a flip phone, open, close, open, close. The agonizing forward movement seemed pointless, draining the energy from my body in slow motion. The water filling the gap at the top of the wetsuit with each dip below the surface now enveloped my arms and legs, increasing the weight I dragged through the water.

As my exhaustion grew, I struggled to stay above water. A mouthful of salt-water gagged me. I coughed and sank. I bobbed up and again sank down. More coughing. *Is this really happening?* I dug inside myself for mental strength.

Ten minutes after the conflict began, I saw Susan progressing. *If she can make it, I can.* The comforting four-foot gap between us now extended back to eight feet. She was eight—now ten—feet closer to shore than me, her black mass surfacing like a whale or a shark.

Seeing twenty feet of water still between me and rest, isolation weighed me down as much as the incoming water. *I'm alone out here.* I timed inhales with desperate lifts from passing swells to avoid more salt-water intake. Rise. Breath. Sink. Repeat.

Several minutes later during a wave boost, I saw Susan crawl onto the beach and collapse near a pile of brown seaweed. In a split-second I recognized she'd made it. I bore no surprise or resentment she beat me . . . again.

After catching her breath, she rose to all fours to cheer me on.

"Come on, Liz, you can do it. Keep going," she said as she climbed to her feet.

"I don't know if I can make it." My voice sounded fatigued, like my body.

"BAFF, you have to make it!" She pleaded.

"I'm so tired . . . " I paddled.

"I NEED you to make it. Keep swimming." Her voice caught. Our eyes met and held.

Ten yards of water loomed ahead. My arms and legs drooped with the saltwater still invading the wetsuit. Both my battle and the ocean continued raging, now thirty minutes since I dove in. I could tap the ocean floor with my feet, but the undertow toward sea cancelled my forward motion.

I leapt.

Then a wave crashed at my back, propelling me toward land. Another wave. Five feet away. With each new wave nudging me onward and upward, the weight of the water in my wetsuit encumbered me more. I dropped to hands and feet and mustered my remaining energy to crawl my way to safety.

I flopped on the sand next to Susan, grateful to be on land. Without speaking she tugged the tight ankle bands of my wetsuit, first one leg then the other, draining a gallon of sea water, popping my puffed-up Michelin Man costume.

After a few minutes I sat upright beside Susan and faced the ocean, reflecting on the terrifying experience. "We could have drowned," I said. She nodded, looking at me with tears in her eyes. We hugged for a long time.

We later discovered we'd been in a dangerous rip current. A rip current is a powerful channel of fast-moving water—often moving faster than an Olympic swimmer—travelling swiftly back toward the sea in an ongoing loop. We should have swum parallel to land to escape its force.

I still love the ocean—and Susan and I are still best friends—but now I respect it and realize it's not just my playground, but a force of nature. The sea stole some of my childhood innocence, forcing me to face harsh realities of life: rip currents and challenges exist, ready or not.

I faced death that day and survived. I learned to surf the waves tossed at me in life, breathe through the struggles, persevere through the exhausting seasons, and walk out a survivor. My greatest youthful realization that daunting afternoon is that situations might not always unfold the way we expect or imagine, but we're stronger than we know. We can choose to swim our way through our trials in life . . . or let them pull us under.

Foretokens

KAY KRATTLI- CENTRAL COAST WRITERS

I have brought you old flowers,
almost spent with pleasure,
each petal curling outward
as far as the stem will allow

The colors are as gentle as
the first languid light of day,
pearl and rose and gold.
Softness reigns on each bowed head

I brought you vibrant young
flowers, glorious in their uprightness,
when our love was a seedling

Now I bend toward you and
love the ripeness in us,
how we have used ourselves
unfurling the best in each other

I have brought you old flowers.
Cherish what remains to them,
they exult fading beauty,
these harbingers of our splendid autumn.

Earth Song: A Cento

ANNE MARIE WENZEL - SAN FRANCISCO PENINSULA

Each long day pulls from the one before,
Moments from yesterday and a century ago—
Some things are simple.

Like a forest fire in a jungle
with no one to watch it
history is a living weapon in yr hand.

The earth wakes up and moans
weeping mad torrents of tears into the river's cold bed.
The rivers can run with blood

and future eclipses will look like this:
a small black pupil in the eye of the sun.
The old women will rise with the moon.

They come and they go. Again they come and they go all night.
I called softly to you so you could choose
not to answer—then called again.

Come down from the green mountains in the darkness.
The aroma of bay leaves blankets the forest,
air unmoving, stillness leaning toward perfect quiet.

Now the earth chants back the sun, splinters the ice.
Breathing correctly keeps you floating. Dress up, dress down.
You will love again the stranger that was yourself.

Now I see the possibilities
are golden dresses in a nutshell.
I raise my hand and continue on alone.

Sources for the cento, by line:
    1. Kiki Petrosino, "Persephone"
    2. Czeslaw Milosz, "Late Ripeness"
    3. David Smith-Ferri, "Adagio"
    4-5. John Ashberry, "The Situation Upstairs"
    6. Diane di Prima, "Rant"
    7. Czeslaw Milosz, "Song on Porcelain"
    8. Arturo Giovannitti, "Mountains"
    9. Ian Davidson, "Lump and Bumps"
    10-11. Dorianne Laux, "Facts About the Moon"
    12.Donna de la Perrière, "Mère"
    13. Arturo Giovannitti, "The Walker"
    14-15. Rita Dove, "Happenstance"
    16. James Wright, "To the Evening Star: Central
       Minnesota"
    17-18. Peter Neil Carroll, "Many Good Ways"
    19. Caroline Goodwin, "Kodiak Herbal"
    20. Anne Matthews, "Year 2"
    21. Derek Walcott, "Love after Love"
    22-23. Rita Dove, "This Life"
    24. Peter Neil Carroll, "Comrades"

ʻŌhiʻa Lehua in a Kīpuka on Hawaiʻi Island

CECILIA JOHANSEN - BERKELEY

A single ʻōhiʻa lehua tree, deeply rooted in a kīpuka,
surrounded by desolation, was not yet beaten.
Its closest kin at a distance.
Curled lava lips chew at the land, red hot, steaming as it goes.
Fiery breath burning and covering low-lying lichen and ferns
turning brown, black, knuckling under,
buried in a puff of flame
dispersed spores no longer required

Lonely ʻōhiʻa, standing, waiting, pondering its fate
watching friends, relatives at a distance.
Heat too strong, inflamed, devoured,
hollow vertical lava tubes to remain a memory.

Waiting, always waiting, destruction all around.
Does it think:
Where can I go?
What can I do?
Will salvation come?

Spit and crackle, licking at kīpuka edges
Devouring, always devouring.
Lava moves like lava
slow as molasses
slow as glacier melt.
Spreading, always spreading
down to the sea.

Scalding days, icy nights,
sluggish lava looks for an easier path
unable to beat the kīpuka.
Annoyed, rushes in a molten tube past the barrier
and its intended victim
only to show up as steam at the edge of the sea.

Danger passed.
Sorrow for loss of its mates on
the black crusty river of doom.

Wait! What is this?
A crimson and black ʻapapane in its branches, long tongue
slurping, sucking, drinking lehua blossom nectar.
What eternal joy!
Life goes on in the
ʻohiʻa's kīpuka.

ʻohiʻa lehua: *Metrosideros macropus*
kīpuka: a clear place or oasis within a lava bed where there
may be vegetation

Mama's Voice

TERESA CONNELLY - FREMONT AREA WRITERS

Low and sweet, Mama called, "Honey Bee." Her rocker gave a satisfying squeak.

Collette pulled her ponytail tighter as she stepped through the screen door. She patted the old woman's shoulder. "You need something?"

Mama laid her hand on top of her daughter-in-law's. "Water?"

"Lots of ice?" Collette used the dish towel she'd slung over her shoulder to wipe away the layer of sweat on Mama's forehead.

"Yep. And some lemon bar if we got any."

Collette chuckled. "For you, I'd walk ten miles into town to get one."

No sooner had the door swung shut behind Collette than Mama resumed rocking and humming in that special way of hers, the way that said to hurry up 'cause I don't have much time left.

Even though her husband had died a while back, Collette didn't mind caring for Mama. Collette had thought the woman would hate her for taking away her only son when they married, but instead Mama had showered her with kindness. When Matthew brought her to meet Mama, Collette was immediately drawn into the biggest hug.

From the beginning Mama insisted on being called just that. Not Mrs. Trevors or Mother or Mom. Just Mama. It made her all the more endearing since no blood connected them.

On top of that, Mama had grace. It didn't matter how ragged her dress, she insisted that it be crisply pressed. And each of her dresses had a hat that, in Mama's mind, was a perfect match. In her younger years Mama loved nothing more than getting a new hat. Some of her favorites had feathers and some had ribbons and even though Collette couldn't see the difference, Mama knew which hat went with which dress and that was that.

Whenever Collette and Matthew had visited, while her husband worked on the house, Collette drove Mama into town. Mama was a proud woman, always walking with her head high and back straight as steel. Collette heard the gossipers whispering a bit too loudly about how Mama pretended she'd come from money. That she'd married down, a not uncommon story out here in the woods.

Truth is, Mama's daddy had been nothing but a tenant farmer who moved the family from one rich man's land to another's. Mama once told Collette about the year they lived in a horse barn because that's where the boss told them to go. It stank in the baking summers and in the winter their breath froze as they huddled under layers of blankets. Mama declared that since she'd been with family, it didn't matter.

Despite everything she'd experienced and lost, Mama was kind to everyone, no matter what they looked like or where they came from. She'd feed neighbors on her porch, sharing what little she had. That's just how Mama was. Collette respected that about the woman.

"I got your water," Collette said as she set the glass on the rickety table next to Mama's chair. "Your lemon bar is right here, too." Exhausted from washing up the kitchen, Collette fell into an empty rocker, the one Papa used way back when.

"Did you make this?" Mama asked after swallowing a bite.

"Just this morning." Collette picked up the newspaper, the one she'd read and carried outside, and used it to fan herself, the pages rustling like autumn's leaves.

"Delicious," Mama said in that not-quite-southern twang of hers. She took a gulp of water and shivered as it went down. "I love me some cold water when it's hot." She returned the glass to its coaster, one with a faded picture of Bill's garage, a freebee from twenty years ago.

Mama closed her eyes, leaned back and rocked. She hummed a tune that Collette thought she remembered.

"Is that 'The Old Wooden Cross'?"

"Rugged. It's Rugged Cross. Much more meaning to it." Mama burst into song in the deep alto that used to fill the church every Sunday morning back when she still went:

"On a hill far away, stood an old rugged cross
The emblem of suff'ring and shame."

Mama's eyes opened wide as tears began to run. "I forget the rest of the words."

"It's okay. You still have your songbook from church, right?"

"Yep. On my dresser."

"Tell you what, after I rest a bit, I'll get it." Mama's right knee started bouncing, a sure sign that the woman was upset. Collette pressed gently until the leg was still. "We can sing later, if you're still up to it."

Mama turned her wrinkled face toward her daughter-in-law and said, "Most days I don't recall your name, and half the time I don't know mine."

"I'm Collette. I married Matthew, your son."

Mama scrunched her cheeks nearly up to her eyes. Shook her head. "I don't have no daughter-in-law and I don't know no Matthew."

Collette sighed. More and more Mama's memory was sputtering. She scooted her chair closer and rested her arm across the woman's shoulders. "Matthew would have been fifty this year. I miss him."

After an uncomfortable period of silence, Mama nodded. "I remember him." She tapped her forehead. "Tall man. Soft voice."

"That was Papa," Collette said. "Matthew was tall, alright, but his voice was deep like a well."

Mama reached for the lemon bar and took one nibble after another until the last bite was gone. "Can I have more?"

"Tomorrow."

Mama sighed a deep, soul-shattering sound. Suddenly she shot up straight, and with wide-open eyes, said, "Is tomorrow Sunday? If'n it is, I'd like to go to church. I haven't been since Matthew died because I can't bear walking the same places he walked."

"I'll take you if you want."

Mama's face lit up brighter than the sun. "That'd be nice. I need to reckon myself to the Lord."

"You got nothing to be sorry for," Collette said.

Mama pushed herself up out of the rocker and then leaning on her cane a little too much for Collette's comfort, toddled inside. "I got to get myself ready 'cause I believe Preacher Davis will be speaking. Oh, I love the way that man calls on the Lord."

Collette grabbed the dishes because she couldn't leave nothing outside unless she wanted raccoons and stray cats coming around. As she headed toward the kitchen she listened for the tap-tap of the cane. When the sound turned left, Collette knew that Mama found the correct room. Collette wondered what the woman was up to. She never knew, because sometimes Mama meant to use the bathroom but took a nap instead. That created another mess for Collette to deal with.

As Collette rinsed the dishes, she thought about how long it had been since she went to church. Not since Matthew died. It wasn't because of a loss of faith, but because being in the building where they got married and spent Sundays listening to Mama sing in the choir would have brought up too many memories. Some good, some not. But, if Mama wanted to go, they'd be there bright and early the next day.

Collette pulled a chicken out of the refrigerator and washed it off. After cutting it in pieces she stuck half in the freezer. Rubbed the rest with a mesquite marinade, bagged them, and put them in the fridge. She shucked an ear of corn and peeled a potato. She disliked potatoes, but Mama insisted it wasn't a proper meal without spuds in some form or other. Collette decided she'd bake them so she could control how much sour cream landed on her mother-in-law's.

"Look," Mama said as she flounced into the kitchen. "Folks haven't seen me in ages. Want to make a good impression." She held the skirt out wide. "What do you think?"

Collette remembered Mama wearing that dress to a Fourth of July Picnic at First Baptist six years ago. It fit beautifully then, but now it hung a bit loose. Back then the colors were crisp and bright, but now it was faded, but the pride in Mama's voice kept Collette's mouth shut. She barely held back a snicker at the old-fashioned hat perched on Mama's head because she knew the woman wouldn't leave home without it. "You look great."

"My husband Gerald bought this in Kansas City. Every time he traveled, he returned with something: hats, dresses or sparkly jewelry. When I asked where he got the money, instead of telling, he'd wrap me in his arms so tight I could barely breathe."

"That's nice." Collette was surprised with all those words flowing out considering that Mama normally only mumbled a sentence or two.

"Gerald never told me. Claimed it would spoil the surprise."

When Mama's shoulders sagged, Collette grabbed the woman around the waist and turned her toward the hall. "Time to change back." In the bedroom Collette pulled the dress over Mama's head and then hung it on a hook on the backside of the door. She slid a clean shift down the woman's arms, then tied on the eyelet apron that Mama loved.

"When I smelled perfume on him, I knew he was cheating. He didn't deny it. Just picked up his traveling bag, and when that door slammed behind him, I yelled to never come back."

Collette brushed Mama's frizzy gray hair. She worked as gently as possible, trying to protect Mama's tender scalp.

"Why you using that god-awful thing?" Mama said. "I like me a good, stiff brushing."

"It's like a massage. Close your eyes and relax."

She wrinkled her nose and whined, "I don't like it."

Collette pulled hairs off the bristles and dropped them in the trash can. "How about you go sit in your rocker?"

Mama hummed as they trundled down the hall, another song Collette knew. When Mama sang, "Amazing grace how sweet the sound ..." in her rich alto Collette harmonized beautifully, taking the soprano line. Like always, it ended when Mama lost the words.

No sooner was Mama settled with a blanket on her lap, than she fell asleep.

Collette knew now was a good time to pull the laundry off the line. She didn't like to leave Mama's threadbare clothes out for the world to see any longer than necessary. It wasn't because no one else hung clothes up to dry. Every yard in the Sterling Mobile Home Park displayed faded and ragged remnants of cheap, store-bought, hand-me-down clothes.

At least Mama's house wasn't in the worst condition, thanks to all the work Matthew had done. The neighbor across the street, Joe Maxwell, his siding was peeling off and Pete Smith, the old man next door, his windows were covered with tattered plastic that no longer kept out bugs.

Two years before they'd known Matthew was dying, he'd replaced all the cracked windows and updated the appliances. He'd installed an air conditioner in the front room and another in Mama's bedroom which didn't make that big of a difference on hot, humid days, but it pleased Mama nonetheless.

Mama was asleep when Collette carried the clothes inside. She watched a news show while she folded the laundry. Nothing happening other than sadness and misery. Just like here in this neighborhood. One after another, the old ones were dying off. Sooner or later, Mama would join them.

When she finished, she put Mama's clothes in her dresser, then her own into the suitcase because there wasn't anywhere else to put them.

After checking on Mama, Collette crept down the steps, missing the creaky parts. She fired up the gas barbeque Matthew had given Mama one Christmas. Thank goodness Collette had a new tank delivered recently or she would have had to use the oven.

She knew her cooking skills were limited. Her own mama had tried to teach her, but gave up because all Collette wanted to do was read. School work. But when she could get to the library, she checked out books about horses or stories that happened somewhere she'd most likely never go.

When she shared an apartment with friends, they rotated the cooking, a problem until Collette found an easy recipe book at a thrift store. She used it now just to get by.

Once the chicken had started cooking, and seeing Mama still asleep, Collette went inside to finish up. She set plates and silverware on the table, dished up the salad, and dressed the potato.

When she opened the door, Collette saw that Mama was still asleep. Troubling, but she didn't wake her because Mama didn't sleep well at night.

Collette had moved in when Mama needed supervision. There was no money for hired help, and Mama didn't want strangers in her house. That left Collette.

She had to get Mama to the bathroom, or there'd be problems. Could already be problems as it had been a while since she'd gone. Collette wiped her hands, took a deep breath then went outside.

As soon as she really looked at her mother-in-law, Collette realized that the tilt of Mama's head wasn't right. It leaned so far to the left that it looked as if someone'd snapped it right off. And her left arm hung over the chair's arm, fingers loose. Collette had never seen Mama like that.

"You okay?" She wasn't and Collette knew it as soon as she felt her arm. What little medicine she understood came from TV, but that was enough.

The woman on the porch, that person leaning over the rocker's arm, wasn't Mama. No pretty tune emanated from her lips, no singing "Precious Lord" in that delicious voice of hers. No spark. Nothing.

Collette picked up Mama's hand and rubbed the palm. "I guess your time's come. Too bad you'll miss church tomorrow."

Sobs broke loose, the loud racking kind of hurt so deep it's hard coming back. When the sun chose that moment to heat up her tear-streaked face, Collette sensed that despite her grief, everything would be okay.

She watched a flock of starlings swirl in massive streaks of black. They'd been Mama's favorite because, as she'd said, "Them birds are like people. They run in crazy circles, doing the same thing over and over expecting different results even though it ain't gonna happen."

Collette was going to miss Mama. In times of trouble the woman had sung songs of love and redemption. "Jesus Loves Me" was a favorite. Collette closed her eyes and imagined Mama's rich alto belting out:

Jesus loves me! This I know,
For the Bible tells me so;
Little ones to Him belong;
They are weak, but He is strong.

Even though Mama was happily off in that home Jesus had waiting for her, Collette would miss her. No more late night bathroom runs. No more stories about people she'd never known. No more hearing her precious Mama's voice.

She went inside to call the sheriff. Next week, once Mama was taken care of, she'd close up her suitcase and drive home, back through the winding roads that got her here.

The Tie that Bound

SHIRLEY PETRO-TIMURA - INLAND EMPIRE

A teen boy ran by with winged feet,
intent on getting over the train tracks to see Bonnie.
The winds carried a flow
that whipped raven black hair
back into the deep.

I sat in the steel tube as before me fell a blinking gate,
gazing at the strong body aching to feel
the rumble, the essence of infinity.
Now a boy who will not be late.

The bar skimmed his side,
the sneakers were tied so tight.
Shiny new ones, so trendy, had to be so right.
With laces too long.
One tangled in the track nail!

He kneeled to genuflect for mercy,
tugging the shoe off...a fail.
I got out to aid an escape.
His eyes hollowed, his mouth an Edvard Munch gape.
My face now
covered with blood and bone.
Going home...gone home.

"Yes, Dear."
SHAWN LANGWELL - REDWOOD WRITERS

As Grandpa picked at a sore on his big toe
we got to talking about life and such.

He did most of the talking, from a gray recliner,
me listening intently on brown shag carpet,
near his feet, while he talked, or so I recall.

We swapped fond memories
and he—tales of regret—
and things that nagged at him
more than his infected foot.

"I don't know how much longer I'll be here,"
he remarked out of the blue.

His words felt like a sucker punch,
or that time, when I was ten, when
Larry Frazier unexpectedly kneed me in the nuts.

"What do you mean?" I asked,
not sure I wanted to hear the answer.

"You never want to plant your roots too deep," said he,
pulling at the tab of blood-stained, dry skin.

"I felt really bad leaving them like that...
I was young and scared," he continued—no, mumbled—
chin pinned to his chest.

"Leaving who? What do you mean?"

"I had a daughter and got married young but left them—
her name was Ruth. She's got to be about forty-five now.

His eyes glassy, wandered to the far corner
of the paneled living room as he continued.

"But I'm sure glad I met your grandma. We've had a good life.
I'm sorry your dad couldn't be there for you boys,
but we're so proud of you."

Sensing this may be the last time I might see him alive,
an invisible ripcord appeared inside my tightening chest,
imploring me to ask,
"Besides never planting your roots too deep,
what other advice would you give to me?"

"Yes, Dear," was all he said.

I raised my eyebrows. "Huh?"

Grandpa, wearing a wry smile,
nodded toward my grandma slaving away
in the tiny mobile home kitchen,
making fried okra and shrimp gumbo for supper.

As if on cue, she sweetly hollered,
"Em, can you take out the trash?"

What else could he say?
but two simple words spoken with love:

"Yes, Dear."

Mary Agnes McKinley

MARLENE AUGUSTINE-GARDINI - REDWOOD WRITERS

Mary Agnes McKinley walked out of Dempsey's bar and dropped dead. It wasn't unusual for Mary Agnes to be in a bar. Or to be drunk. Or to fall down. However, she always managed to get up and stagger down the road. This time she was dead. Not dead drunk. Just dead.

Mickey The Smoker and Curley Dan heard the thump, got up from their stools, and looked out the door.

"Mary Agnes," Mickey said.

"Can see that," Dan replied. "Think she's OK?"

"Don't think so. Not the way her eyes are, like opened and not blinkin' like that."

They stared at her, watching her not breathe.

"Damn, Mickey. Shoulda we tell Dempsey? Folks won't be able to get in with her all sprawled out like that in front of the door."

"Might better," Mickey said.

Dempsey came to the door. Looked down at Mary Agnes and shook his head.

"Ah, Mary, Mary." He dabbed at his eyes with a bar towel and turned to call the police. He looked from Mickey to Dan and back again.

"Don't you derelicts touch her or *anything* on her, ya hear me? You leave her be till they come, got me?"

They nodded without taking their eyes off Mary Agnes.

Sirens blared. In minutes the police and the coroner were walking around Mary Agnes and mumbling to each other. Mickey and Dan stood off to the side and watched. When the coroner finally nodded and a gurney was brought out to load Mary Agnes, they both sighed heavily in unison.

"She was a good girl," Mickey said wiping off a sniffle with a nicotine-stained finger. "Always willin' to share if ya didn't got nothin' and she did."

"Yeah," Dan said clearing the lump in his throat. "She never tried to cross ya or take your bottle if ya passed out. Didn't say much that made sense, though. She always seemed to be watchin' everything that was going on, muttering about plots, plots, plots. I always wondered if she was worried about where she'd be buried. Now she don't gotta worry no more, I guess".

They stood watching the people with plastic gloves and coveralls arrange Mary Agnes on her back, close her eyes, and load her onto the gurney.

"Know where her cart is at?" Mickey said looking around as the doors of the dead people's van closed on Mary Agnes.

"Over on Fifth. Behind the old Denny's, by the dumpster".

They watched as the van headed north. They linked arms not so much in camaraderie as to maintain an upright position, and made their way south to Fifth Street.

"It's there," Dan said, pointing to the corner of a rusty shopping cart tucked behind a dumpster. It was carefully covered with a faded, yet remarkably clean, red Pendleton blanket.

They wheeled it out, took off the blanket, and stared at the contents. Everything was neatly arranged in clear plastic boxes. A fork, knife, and spoon rested with a chipped plate and ceramic mug which read "SF GIANTS." There was a stack of clean paper napkins from McDonald's alongside small packets of ketchup and mustard and two cardboard containers of salt and pepper. Another box held two XL sweaters; one pair of folded jeans, size 14; two pairs of women's underpants and four socks. A small box held toothpaste, a toothbrush, four small bottles of hotel shampoo and hair conditioner, and a brush with almost all the bristles intact. A large, green plastic bag held a rain slicker, matches in a Ziploc baggie, and some folded-up dry newspaper.

Mickey and Dan took each box out, looking at everything.

"Mary Agnes had, like, a little house here, huh?" Dan said, staring at the plastic boxes lined up in front of them.

"Yep," Mickey said, reaching in for the largest box in the bottom of the cart.

"Huh ...Look at this!"

They stared at the books resting one on top of the other. Most were worn and dog-eared, but a few looked relatively new.

"I didn't know Mary Agnes was one of those smart readin'-type people. I never saw her with a book in the bars, I don't think." Dan picked up the top book.

"*The Best Short Stories of 1986*," he read slowly.

Mickey looked over Dan's shoulder at the other titles.

"Looks like she got a lot of these for other years, too. Guess she liked to read this stuff. Go figure. Never been one for reading myself," Mickey said. "Seemed a waste of time when there was so much livin' to actually do."

Dan nodded. "What we gonna do with this stuff, do ya think? I'd kinda like to keep the kitchen and that hair stuff. "Specially that brush. Looks almost new, huh?"

Mickey looked at the plastic boxes laid out before them like clear glass coffins.

"Well, I say you take what ya want. I'll take the blanket and the cart. And we can use the other stuff to trade for some drink. But those books, nobody'll want 'em. I say we leave 'em. But let's take the box. Somebody'll want that, for sure."

"Thank ya, Mary Agnes! You were a fine woman, even if ya were a strange one!"

They each took an edge of the book box, flipped it upside down, spilling the books onto the alley. They loaded the rest of the boxes in the cart and made their way back to Dempsey's.

The night fog seeped in. Winds swirled down Market Street and whipped around the corners of alley ways. The pages of the books dumped on the stones flipped open in the wind, flicking up the names of authors celebrated in the collections of The Best Short Stories of each year. And the name Mary Agnes McKinley appeared in every book and soaked up the rain like a drunk tasting her last drink.

Mom's Last Ride

ROSE OWENS - TRI-VALLEY WRITERS

"**H**ow are you doing back there, Mom? Comfortable? Too bumpy?"

No answer. But I didn't expect one. For the first time in my life, I could string two sentences together without being interrupted. I glanced through the window behind me. The interior of my camper shell was shadowed, but I could see Mom's casket bounce up and down. It wasn't that this was a rough road— just the almost non-existent shock absorbers on my truck.

I loved this old truck despite its idiosyncrasies. Mom didn't.

"Suzie, why'd you waste your money on this rattletrap? You sure got cheated." I winced. Mom was gone, but her voice still echoed in my head.

"Mom, it's a good truck. It just needs a little work," I muttered. "Dad taught me how to fix trucks, remember?"

"No good. That's what Daniel Tolliver was. Encouraged you in your foolish tomboy ways. No way to treat a seventeen-year-old girl."

I shook my head. I wasn't about to let her run my beloved father down—even if I was only remembering her often-repeated refrain. I clenched the steering wheel tighter and focused on the road ahead. It had been a long trip—driving from California to Utah by myself was a challenge—but had I been alone? Dead or not, she still nagged, criticized, and disagreed with me. I loved her, but that didn't change the facts. She knew she was always right and didn't hesitate to tell me so.

Dad taught me to keep my word—always. He promised me he would always love me. So why did he have to die the week before we planned to move from Taylorsville, Utah, to San Francisco? We buried him in the family plot beside his deceased father-in-law and moved anyway. Didn't have a choice. House was already sold.

Ten years later, when Mom got the cancer diagnosis, she wanted promises from me. "Promise me that you'll bury me beside Daniel. A woman belongs beside her husband."

I tried to use logic to wiggle out of promising. "Are you sure you want to be in that plot?" I asked. "Mona will be buried there. You've always hated your mother-in-law and you want to be near her?"

Mom was adamant. "I want to be buried by Daniel."

I grimaced but nodded my head.

"Promise me that you'll bury me in my green polka dot dress."

I groaned. That dress made her look ghastly.

"And I want my yellow hat. The one with the red rose on the brim."

"Really, Mom? Are you sure?"

"Yes," she snapped. "Promise me. You wouldn't deny a sick woman her dying wishes, would you?"

My mind said, *Yes, I would.* But my voice said, "Yes, Mom, I promise."

I glanced back at the casket again. "Mom, you didn't think things through, did you? Just like always. If you wanted to be buried in Utah, you should have arranged to die there."

I gripped the steering wheel tighter and stared at the twisting road ahead. "Did you know it would cost almost two thousand dollars for the funeral home to transport you back to Utah? Two thousand dollars that I don't have. You said there was money in the bank to pay for your funeral. Hah! Your savings account had a measly four thousand. The mortuary charged me $325 to come get you after you died. Embalming was $725. Hairstyling and makeup were $250. Then the funeral home tacked on a $2,000 basic services fee—non-negotiable, they said. And I'm stuck with your medical bills."

I squinted at the road sign I was approaching: Taylorsville 30 miles. "We're almost there. Sorry about the casket, Mom. I didn't have the two thousand the mortuary wanted for the economy model. I bought one from Walmart for half as much. Your money's all gone. How was I going to come up with the money to transport you back to Utah?" I shook my head. "Sorry, Mom. I almost gave up and had you cremated. But then Monty said that if I got a permit, I could drive you to Utah. That permit only cost twelve dollars. Saved me $1,988. And you get a ride in my truck."

I smiled. "Remember the day I brought my truck home? You refused to go for a ride in Betsy."

"It's ridiculous to name a truck. And that truck's a rattletrap. Riding in it would be a death wish come true."

"That's right, Mom. Just like always, you're right. You got your death wish. You get your first ride in my truck—and your last one."

I looked at my watch. About twenty-five miles to the Fairview Cemetery. I would be on time—just barely. The cemetery man had been very specific with his instructions. "Casket has to be sealed and labeled with the deceased's name. We can't store the deceased, so you need to arrive one hour before the service—no earlier and no later."

This trip hadn't been easy. Old Betsy had been finicky. Sometimes I had to turn the key five or six times before she would start. One time I flooded the engine and was stuck for half an hour.

Having a flat tire hadn't helped either. A cute guy stopped and offered to help. No way was I going to let him see the casket in the back of my truck. I stuck my nose up in the air and said, "I'll be fine. I'm not helpless. Don't worry about me."

"Have it your way," he muttered, He got back in his Prius and drove away.

"He was really cute, Mom," I said. "And I wished I'd let him help. It took me forever to change that tire."

Fifteen miles and things were getting desperate. I really needed to pee. There was no way I could hold out any longer, and I didn't even know if there would be a restroom at that little country cemetery. I saw a service station up ahead.

"We're making a quick stop, Mom. It won't take long."

I pulled right up to the door of the outside restroom. My fingers reached out to turn the engine off. *What if Betsy decides this is the time that she won't start? I'll be late. I'll be stuck with Mom.*

"I'll be fast," I told Mom again. "Don't go away. I'll be right back." I laughed as I hopped out of the truck and rushed into the restroom. I was washing my hands when I heard Betsy roar away. I swung the door open and watched my truck disappear down the road.

I waited fifteen minutes for the police to arrive.

"My truck was stolen. You need to get it back. Now."

"Hold on, Missy." The officer flashed a tolerant smile at me. "We need to fill out the paperwork. It won't take long." He waved a clipboard with several pages on it as he slowly fished in one pocket and then another for a pen.

"I don't have time to fill out paperwork. Mom's in that truck and I need to get her back."

"So, it's a kidnapping," he said. "That's a different set of paperwork. I'll get it." He turned toward the police car.

"Well, it's not exactly a kidnapping," I said. "More like a body-napping."

"Huh?"

"That guy stole my truck. And my purse. And my mom. She's in her casket in her green polka dot dress and yellow hat—just like I promised." I swiped my hand across my face and gulped. "And I have to get her back so I can bury her by Dad—just like I promised. And the cemetery guy is waiting for me to get there . . . And they can't have a funeral without the body, can they?"

I was falling to pieces, but the words kept spilling out, and I couldn't stop blubbering.

"There, there, Miss . . . Miss?" he said.

"Miss Tolliver, Suzie Tolliver."

"You were heading to the Fairview Cemetery? Why don't I take you there?"

I nodded my head. I scribbled the facts on his paperwork as we drove.

When I stepped out of the police car at the cemetery, a furious man rushed toward me. He bombarded me with words. "It's about time you got here. Your friend just dumped the casket and drove away. Reckless. Careless. You're lucky the casket didn't break. We can start the service in five minutes." He shoved a white rose into my hand.

I looked past him. Mom's casket had been placed above the open grave—right beside Dad's tombstone. The funeral began. I barely heard the words the minister spoke. *Where was Betsy? Would I ever get her back?* I placed my rose on the casket and turned to find the police officer right behind me.

"Miss Tolliver, we've recovered your truck."

"Where?"

"Three miles up the road. The driver crashed it into a tree. He wasn't very coherent. Acted real crazy. Must have been the impact because he wasn't drunk or on drugs. He said there was a voice coming from the back of the truck. A woman kept giving him driving directions, and she yelled at him when he drove past the cemetery. She kept yakking at him until he turned around and came back. He said she was saying that Daniel was waiting for her."

The police officer shook his head. "Near as I can piece it together, the man claims that when he left the cemetery after dumping the coffin, he looked over at the passenger seat. A lady wearing a green polka dot dress was sitting there. An awful red rose on her hat bobbed up and down with every word she spoke. 'Don't drive so fast. Cops like to catch speeders on this road. You'll get a ticket. You're going around this curve too fast.' He said that's when he swerved off the road and hit the tree. We looked, but we couldn't see a lady anywhere. Guess he really banged his head bad. Crazy."

I smiled. Mom always was a backseat driver.

Mr. Reuben

SUE ANDREWS - INLAND EMPIRE

In January 2021, I found myself calling 911. It wasn't my first time calling about my heart, but I thought it might be my last. My blood pressure had skyrocketed to 200/110 (normal is 120/70.)

"I'm scared to go the hospital," I told my husband, Ken, while we waited for the ambulance.

"Why?" he said. "You've never been before."

"It'll be different this time. I'll be alone . . . Remember what happened to Tina and Kathleen?" He knew those girlfriends were two of the many friends we had lost the previous year due to COVID. He understood my inference.

Ken looked at me. "Don't worry. That's not going to happen to you."

He tried to be encouraging, but I couldn't get the thought out of my mind. *Will I be just like Tina and Kathleen whose spouses could not be with them in the hospital?* Before the ambulance took me away, I hugged and kissed my husband as though it would be our last.

I was still crying, thinking these terrible thoughts, when they put me in the hospital's holding room with my attending paramedic team. Over the next seven hours, they were able to lower and stabilize my blood pressure.

By evening, staff put me in a wheelchair and rolled me to the triage center where a nurse took my vitals, and a tech gave me an x-ray. Afterwards I was pushed to the ER waiting area.

It was getting late and the battery on my phone was running low. I had no charger with me. My lightweight clothes became less warm with the evening breeze whooshing in each time the sliding glass doors opened with a new patient. No one had given me anything to eat or drink. I became scared.

I trembled thinking I might die alone. I called my husband, trying to compose myself. "Honey, could you please come over with my charger, a sweatshirt, and something to eat? I've had nothing all day."

"I'll get there as fast as I can, but you know they won't let me in."

"I know, honey, I know. Just do what you can and come quickly!"

After that phone call and hearing the sound of his voice, I burst into tears. I had a horrible feeling of abandonment and dread. His words, "they won't let me in," made me shiver. *Will I be like my friends who never saw their spouses alive again? Was this morning the last time I ever saw his face or kissed his lips?* It brought me some solace to remember what I had told him. I love you. You are the best husband in the world. You gave me the best years of my life.

It was six in the evening when staff exchanged the wheelchair for a hospital bed and moved me to an ER room. *Finally, those medications should let me get some rest.* I stretched my legs in the bed and tried to relax. I had just closed my eyes when a staff member pulled back my curtain and handed me a large brown shopping bag.

"I have something for you," he said. "I think it's from your husband who just dropped it off."

"Yes," I said, smiling for the first time all day. I opened the bag. "I'm sure it is."

I looked in the bag and found everything I'd requested. A charger for my phone. A sweatshirt to keep me warm. Plus, my favorite sandwich. My husband, the chef in the family, had read my mind. I had been thinking about those Reuben sandwiches he had made the night before.

If this were to be my last meal, I wouldn't have selected anything different. When I unwrapped the cellophane, it was still *warm!* I tasted the first bite thinking I'd died and gone to heaven.

* * *

Once safe at home in my own bed days later, I realized how foolish it was of me to start planning my own obituary. My husband was right, nothing had happened to me. I had survived and made it through the ordeal.

After eating one of my favorite dishes again, I couldn't stop obsessing about that Reuben. My husband had put time, love, and effort into making that hospital sandwich. I had already honored Ken with my love and appreciation, but felt it was the sandwich's turn. Writing an obituary for it instead of my own, made me laugh out loud. I had to write an obit story because the Reuben I had eaten had died, not me.

I thought about all the components of my so-called last meal. It amazed me that so many different ingredients from many countries made it so mouthwatering. When the ideas came to my mind, it still made me smile while writing a sandwich obituary. What would those ingredients have said at the memorial?

The two Russian constituents told the story of how they had gathered and sandwiched everyone together. They both loved their maker, Captain Rye, who had kneaded them into existence. He had baked them until they formed a hard crust with the exact number of caraway seeds in the soft, chewy center. Baker Captain Rye knew exactly when to take his delicacy out of the oven so that the total flavor commanded a delectable experience.

The creamy Swiss duo, the holey men of the gathering, came next and explained how they had stuck together until the bitten end. I must say, I thought that descriptor was apropos. I devoured that simple meal as if it *had* been my last.

The German felt he had to defend his involvement and contribution. He described how his journey had taken the longest route. First, he had started out as a cabbage, then someone pickled him in vinegar to become sauerkraut. His maker/baker added extra caraway seeds to make the whole ensemble savory.

The *crème de la crème* of the entire operation was argued by the thick Irishman. He clarified that if it hadn't been for his added layer upon layer of his scrumptious corned beef, cured from a beef brisket, the sandwich would have never been. Not to argue with the Irishman, but I thought everything in this collective cooperative melded into perfection because of everyone's participation.

After that heavenly hospital meal, I remembered saying to myself. *Now I could die happy eating this last meal on Earth.* I am ever so thankful and glad that *my* Maker, my God, determined an obituary was not meant for me.

There was only one obit meant to be written and that was for my favorite sandwich. The one I used to call a plain Reuben, I now give more respect to all who contributed to it. The sandwich will always be called Mr. Reuben to me. May you rest in peace.

My Friend Claudia

NONA SMITH - WRITERS OF THE MENDOCINO COAST

W e held our wine glasses up and tapped their rims together. *Clink.*

Do you know why that's done?" Claudia asked.

"I have no idea," I said.

"The French began the custom centuries ago. It's to make us appreciative of all five of our senses. We observe the rich color of the wine; we put our nose to the glass and inhale, taking in its aroma; we feel the wine on the tongue; then taste it, of course. And with the clinking of glasses, we include our fifth sense."

Claudia had a treasure trove of that kind of information.

"Ahhh, les Francais; ils savent tout," she added.

She spoke three languages fluently and had enough vocabulary in others to order wine in restaurants and find bathrooms in foreign countries. Born in Germany and well-travelled, Claudia had European sensibilities and a sophisticated sense of style. Her hair was cut by a Sassoon-trained stylist, she wore only Italian-made shoes, and the walls of her dining room were painted Chinese red, seasons before that trend appeared in *Architectural Digest*. She owned a few expensive, elegant gold pieces, but most of her jewelry was purchased from local artisans during her travels or at art fairs at home. It was jewelry we bonded over.

On her first day working as a travel agent at Trips Out Travel, I admired her earrings: thumb-nail size, straight-back chairs, crafted from black metal. Definitely not gold, but certainly expensive. Something she might have found in a museum gift shop.

My compliment caused her to tuck a strand of red hair behind her ear and caress her earlobe. "I found them in Taormina. I had to sort through all that cameo crap they sell tourists before I found anything interesting."

Claudia had opinions. Very firm opinions. About almost everything, but especially about food, and clothing, and what was worth spending money on. Her generous smile drew people to her; her sharp tongue sent them away. She possessed a quirky, wicked sense of humor and had a flare for the dramatic. She had once been married and had a son, Adam, she adored, but when I met her, Claudia was living alone in a one-bedroom gem of a house secreted into the Berkeley hills. She took her cockapoo Milo, a yappy attention-grabbing dog, with her almost everywhere, cradling him like a baby in the crook of her arm.

Claudia was especially devoted to the game of *What If…* What if you weren't a travel agent, what else would you be? What if you didn't live in this country, where else would you like to live? What if you knew how to play a musical instrument really well, which one would it be?

Milo was at the groomers the afternoon we dined at our favorite dim sum restaurant in the city. We'd already polished off a steaming bamboo basket of shrimp dumplings and a platter of *al dente* Chinese broccoli with oyster sauce when Claudia nodded to the server rolling yet another dim sum-laden trolley towards us.

"We'll have the *shu mai* and the pork buns," she said with authority.

We held our wine glasses up and tapped their rims together. *Clink.*

"What if," Claudia began, "you were on death row, and going to order your last meal, what would it be?"

I don't recall what I answered, but Claudia's answer came quickly and definitively. She waved her chopsticks over the bountiful table. "This is what I would order."

Late the next morning, Adam called. "Sit down. It's bad news about Mom. She died yesterday."

"Oh, Adam," I said. Tears sprang to my eyes.

He continued to speak, "...alone in the house...Milo was with her...brain aneurism..."

I heard his words, vaguely, but the picture in my mind was of Claudia, her chopsticks held aloft, pronouncing the dim sum her last meal of choice.

Haiku for Nellie

LEO ARENALES - CENTRAL COAST WRITERS

Nellie's gentle bite
Round with sticky wet delight
Blue ribbon winner

The Truth in Trees

ANTHONY PINO - FREMONT AREA WRITERS

Trees don't lie;
they hold the truth in their rings,

binding old books where we read
the sagas of seed-splitting,

sapling birth, celebrations,
struggles, long, glorious seasons of rain

and screams of wildfires.
Imaged in their bark are

the scarred, mossy faces of old sentinels
who have guarded the woods' secret

minework and protected
its scriptural history.

Walk slowly, and
among the leafy giants

and feathery ferns,
you might hear the quiet recital

of ancient scholarship
and the pipes of faithful service.

A Country Most Dear

JONATHAN PAZER - WRITERS OF THE MENDOCINO COAST

I toss and turn twisted across a
narrow-minded row of airline seats their
pitiless armrests upraised their buckles bared
sleepless in the stormy red-eyed sky

careening toward the Manhattan of my birth
in no good state of mind
I return again for my father's sake
to watch him mourn my mother

she sits beside him on the paisley couch
her grand host of mad soliloquies
all fled now to their unwritten memoirs
and half-read scripts

into this vacuum of wordless loss
and in memorial adoration he conjures a
fantasy of shared silence for the
ingenue of his golden footlights

a revised end to their third act that is
equal parts devotion and emptiness
fragile as fame in her rose-colored nightgown
sunlight filtered through her undyed hair

she still wears my mother's arms
though they hang stiff and vacant in her lap
between those arms once lay
my mother's embrace

a country most dear to me
the beloved homeland to which I can
never again return—not because
I have forsaken or forsworn it

but because it has
shrunk away to
nothing.

What I Saw on My Walk

NATY OSA - WRITERS OF THE MENDOCINO COAST

To ease the unease of the morning news, portents
Of future summers rife with doom, I donned
Glasses and hat, leashed the dog, and took a walk.

I saluted...
A fire hydrant, civil servant sentinel straight, red
Overalls, sky-blue cap ever vigilant as I passed.

Unaware of their heralded fate, berries swaying on a
Bramble pulsed green, amber, red, nature's cyclical
Semaphore. I stopped at a red one to let the time pass.

I saw white tatted doilies of Queen Anne's lace
Poised over a meadow on tall, proud stalks,
A fine tea setting, surely, for a ladybug.
Later birds' nests they'll become.

Black-eyed Susans, aptly called, sunny petals
Open wide, cool along the road-side brook, although
Bristly underneath, are both fetching and demure.
Dandy bachelors button-ed tight in hopeful clusters close by.

A field of hay on Monday swayed in the wind,
Licking at raindrops, today prone stalks like fallen soldiers
Lie felled by the scythe, next week, perhaps, they'll dot
The hillside baled in tight rolls for the cows to admire.

If I had it in my power to distill drop by drop
This Virginia summer day, I would keep it on a shelf
Sealed in a memory jar so that it would not escape,
A seed vault of remembrances to plant later on.

The Swing Set

BRAD HOGE - SAN FRANCISCO PENINSULA

The swing set swayed
more and more

as our children
grew and swung higher.

As the wood grayed
and the bracings oxidized.

It has brittled,
and creaks in the wind.

Webs now seem to hold
it together. As the sun's

heat hardens the exterior,
and water's ravenous

softening from the inside
deceives those looking

at the empty
swings with fondness.

At time frozen
only in the mind.

Near Death by Quicksand
ROBIN GIGOUX - MT. DIABLO

Years ago, recovering from my painful divorce, I made it a point to catch up on some fun. My playful pal Sue and I and a group of friends once rafted on the gentle Truckee River and laughed ourselves silly, competing with each other to see who could stay dry. When Sue suggested whitewater rafting on the Stanislaus River, I was in.

I learned that white water rivers are rated from I to VI in degree of difficulty for guides, or in my mind, risk of physical injury. Rafting on a Class III River with medium-size rapids sounded challenging, yet safe enough. I looked forward to this exciting new experience.

Our group crowded into a room at a weathered motel nearby the night before our day on the river. We stayed up late joking about the weather, the rapids, the rafts, and the guides. Most in our party had whitewater rafted before, but this newbie, while looking forward to the excitement, cringed at the thought of unimaginable rapids. I didn't sleep well.

The next morning, we carpooled to the bus stop. Rickety old busses struggled to transport us upstream to the chaotic launch site, where throngs of eager rafters milled about as guides handed out life jackets to every rider. Other guides handed out lightweight, blue-and-yellow-plastic, paddle-like oars to those who agreed to help steer, if necessary. Many rafters took an oar. Not especially confident I'd be an asset, I didn't.

We then headed to the river and boarded inflated, army green, rubber rafts, each raft capable of holding six to eight riders plus a guide or two. Some riders faced forward straddling the 15-inch inflated rubber rim. Others, like me, sat legs in the raft, facing inward. Guides perched at the back.

Impossible to grip those huge curved sides with hands, guides demonstrated how to "hold on" by slipping our toes into small loops on the flat inside bottom of the raft, one toehold per passenger. More a sense of security than reality, the skill of our guides was expected to keep us in the raft.

"If you should fall out," our guide warned, "ride the water on your back with your toes pointed downriver, and avoid getting stuck in an eddy."

I quivered with dread and exhilaration.

Once informed, our flotilla of thrill seekers hurtled down the river at breakneck speed, guided by the rapid current and skill of the guides, darting through roiling whitewater past semi-submerged rocks, skimming over others, sideswiping downed trees and other vegetation, while tall trees, blue sky, and granite boulders flashed by, all the while being soaked by icy water. Riders cheered surviving the rapids upon arriving at intermittent stretches of calm water.

Halfway down the river, the flotilla stopped for a break at an awesome cave. Rafters had a few minutes to warm up in the sun, wade in tepid, ankle-deep rivulets, or explore the cooler cave. My racing heart had a chance to slow down.

Back on the raging river, a young man and a young woman bounced off our raft as it careened over a submerged boulder and then bumped into a tree stump. The young man broke his ankle when the rushing water forced his leg into an eddy between boulders. A guide from another raft jumped in the river to liberate him. The young woman careened downriver on her back, feet first, as directed. She was rescued in calm water.

I giggled hysterically thinking, *OMG, OMG. I'm going to crack my skull, break my legs, or die!* The roar of the rapids and screams of other people made conversation impossible, leaving me alone with my terror.

At the end of our hours-long, exhilarating journey, guides paddled the rafts into a predetermined disembarkation area, anchoring perpendicular to the bank. Ours, the last raft to anchor downriver, Sue and I disembarked on the downstream side, oddly alone. We were probably joking around when the guides were giving instructions to disembark on the upstream side.

Light-headed with relief that the trip was over and continuing to banter, we stepped into ankle-deep water and onto the silty river bottom, wisecracking about the texture of the muck under our feet, like soft, oily, fireplace soot. The more we sought solid footing, the more we sank, and the harder we laughed. No one saw us and no one heard us shouting for help over the din of the river and the raucous commotion of disembarking people.

Soon up to our armpits in the disgusting river bottom, whether legitimate quicksand or built-up silt, we extended our arms hoping the added resistance would slow us down or stop us. Nope. Facing certain death as we continued to sink into the black and slimy gunk, like birds solidified in flight, helpless and out of options, we laughed hysterically at the absurdity of our situation.

Then came the cavalry. Two bronzed and muscled guides, no doubt counting heads, came around to our side. They quickly produced long boards, readily available for fools like us, laid them over the quicksand—in that bit of water atop the quicksand now licking our chins—and crawled out on their bellies to pull us to safety. The miserable substance intent on sucking us in, Sue sacrificed a shoe.

Once ashore, covered with slime that looked and smelled like rotten vegetation, firepit ash, and stuff I don't want to think about, we were directed to a safe spot along the river to rinse off before boarding the bus. Without soap, the muck clung to our skin, and we stank. Fellow rafters held their noses. Some made faces. Most kept their distance. Sue and I had to laugh at their reactions.

Back at the hotel, Sue and I took long, hot showers and slept well that night. Despite my initial apprehensions, whitewater rafting in the company of my good friend was just what I had needed. I hadn't laughed so much in years.

Chasing Ephemera

STEVE TRENAM - REDWOOD WRITERS

Ansel Adams slept
on the roof of his car,
venturing out on foot
into Death Valley until
the desert sun relented,

and drew a perfect line
down the spine of a sand dune
into his Korona camera.

Galen Rowell stepped off
the bus at twelve thousand feet,
and took off chasing a rainbow,
while his fellow photographers
opted for the warmth of a stove.

Rowell ran until he caught
the rainbow as it streamed down
onto the Dalai Lama's palace.
Camera braced against a post,
he captured more than he saw.

Mark Zukowski, awakened
by a full moon peering
into a Tomales Bay cabin,
donned his robe and waited
for a sonata—
a composition of moonlight
and the glow from a shack
at the end of a pier.

A photograph
that further proves,
artists perpetuate
the fleeting, unrepeatable
moment.

Not My Problem

REBECCA INCH-PARTRIDGE - SACRAMENTO

A hovercar zipped past my vehicle, weaving through the traffic that flowed between the mega-buildings. It nearly collided with the two hovercars ahead of me, then overcorrected and had to veer hard to the right to avoid striking a building. It hit a tree and crashed into the large open courtyard below.

Ah, hell! I'm not stopping just because some idiot got in a wreck. I'm not on duty.

I cut back my thrusters and headed down to assess the situation, all the while wondering why I bothered lying to myself. I always stopped when it looked like a serious accident. *Guess EMS is just in my blood.*

After fifteen years of treating and transporting trauma, paramedicine was more reflex than choice. I landed, jumped out my hovercar, and took in the scene. Thankfully the mega-plex's courtyard had been empty this early in the morning. I approached the downed car, hoping not to deal with any sue-happy patients wanting to make millions by claiming neck pain.

By now, I could see the only occupant of the vehicle. He wasn't moving. *Ah damn! Why'd it have to be an alien?* Even though I'd taken the multi-species certification course, I wasn't comfortable treating non-Humans. There were just too many of them to keep their anatomy and physiology straight. I was always sure I'd end up accidentally treating one of them under the wrong protocol and committing medical aliencide. It was one of the reasons I'd decided to stay on Earth despite the overcrowded condition.

All right, first things first. Airway. Breathing. Circulation.

I probed around his neck where his avian kind should have a pulse. Nothing. But the guy was breathing, and his ice-blue skin hadn't turned the nasty shade of gray that they did when in shock. I reached down to see if I could feel a heartbeat. Instead of humanoid flesh, my hand encountered a rock-like shell.

With the golden wings and skin color of a Sian birdman, but a Prigta exoskeleton, he had to be a Hybrid. Closer inspection revealed his hair to actually be a short cut feline mane of a Katian. And sure enough, when I checked, he had a Katian tail bound to his leg. Only the genetically engineered race known as the Hybrids possessed the traits of so many different species.

I glanced over my shoulder at the crowd gathering around. If anybody recognized what he was, this poor son-of-a-memform would be hauled off to a detention camp.

"You're not my problem. I'm not getting involved," I muttered at the unconscious man. Everybody knew the rumors of how these once-revered Ambassadors and Mediators were treated at the camps. Some even said that the deportation camps never actually deported anyone, but that they executed Hybrids by the hundreds every day. Yet nobody seemed to care.

Both a mobile med-craft and a police siren wailed from not too far away. I noticed a hovercar with a Sian-looking woman and child pull over. The child scrambled to open the door, but the woman yanked him back. She eyed me, looked off in the direction of the sirens, and lifted off.

The police officer reached me before the med-craft. "What ya got, Amber?" she asked.

At first, I feared she remembered me from being on scene together. The bitch and I hadn't exactly gotten along. But she'd just read it off the nametag on my uniform that I hadn't bothered changing out of after shift.

Of all the assholes to show up, why did it have to be her? She was a flaming Humans-First activist. She totally believed all the propaganda blaming his people for everything from the planet-wide depression to the latest flu virus. This "peace" officer had actually bragged about how she helped with the campaign that had led to the entire Hybrid race being outlawed on Earth.

"Single vehicle accident," I told her. "Only one patient. How 'bout getting rid of these lookie-loos, so we can go to work once the rig pulls up?"

She barked orders at the crowd. I turned back to my patient as the med-craft made its descent. His eyes were open and fixed on the back of the officer. Sure the guy belonged to an illegal race, but he didn't deserve to be handed over to her tender mercies.

"I need to check you over for injuries," I said, drawing his attention.

He raised a swollen and bleeding hand in protest. "No, no. That's okay, thank you. I'm not really hurt."

I leaned through the window and into the cockpit, beginning my exam despite his protest. "Listen," I whispered, "you refuse transport, and that cop's gonna wonder why. No Sian could walk away from this crash."

He eyed the passenger door, but it'd been smashed in, preventing any escape. He subtly shifted his eyes to look around the area. I took a guess at what he was looking for. "If your family was following you, your wife had the sense to take off when the cop pulled up."

He stared at me without saying a thing. He tried not to react, but his wings sagged in relief. The intensity of his gaze made me wonder if he was scanning my thoughts. Their ability to read minds was what had led to the Hybrids being convicted of mental rape and banned as a race. But how the hell could *I* know whether this guy was personally guilty of any crimes?

He waited silently to see what I'd do next. With a low growl I explained, "Now if you decide to refuse treatment once you're at the hospital, that's none of my business. And frankly they're so overloaded, I doubt they'd even notice if you just got up and walked away."

He took a calming breath, eyeing me with veiled hope.

What the hell am I doing? I know better than to get involved. I looked back at the med-craft. Pat, one of the new guys from our Emergency Services Department started over with an anti-grav gurney loaded with c-spine, trauma kit, med-box—everything but the birthing roll.

Shit, why couldn't it be someone I know instead of this newbie?

My dour mood brightened when I saw who the newbie was working with. Devin was one of the few medics that didn't think it was beneath him to actually care about the patient.

"You're unconscious," I whispered to my patient. He had the sense to pull a fainting act in case anybody had noticed he'd been awake.

"Hey, Ma," the young and eager newbie said with a grin. I had just met Pat this morning on my way out. Apparently he'd picked up on how everyone called me Ma and liked it . . . a little too much. I'd also made the mistake of saying that I never played Ricky-rescue on my days off. Or in my case Rita-rescue.

"Whatcha got?" he asked.

"Trauma activation. ABCs seem intact. Go get c-spine."

"But I brought it." He pointed to the pile on the anti-grav cot.

"That's not going to work on a Sian, now is it? So go get the inflatable system."

"Yeah. Field stupid-visor's gonna love that," Pat said. I considered telling him that I didn't give a damn what the supervisor loved, but he saw that my temper was about to boil over and added quickly, "Whatever you say, Ma."

I hated that nearly everyone at our department referred to me as Ma. Just because they were all a bunch of kids. And that kid had no right to throw around our vernacular like "stupid-visor" as if he'd been around for years.

Devin moved in to figure out the best way to extricate our patient. The cop came back over and asked how our patient was. "See for yourself," I told her.

"Well, he's under arrest for reckless driving," she responded without emotion.

"If you're going to bind him now, you'll have to ride in with us."

She looked back at her hopped up single-rider craft. "Nah, I'll just meet you down there. I assume you're going to Oakland Trauma Center."

I nodded.

Devin slapped a ventilator on the patient and began his own assessment. It wouldn't be long.

I mentioned to the cop that some of the hovercars were getting too close, trying to get a peek at the show below. She jumped up on her single-rider and motioned them to move back up where they belonged.

I watched her in all her power and glory, muttering, "Yeah, go direct traffic."

By this time, Devin's search for a pulse had become swift professionalism. He snatched the self-adjusting cervical collar from Pat the second he returned, preparing for a rapid extrication. He worked the collar around the Hybrid's neck. "What the hell?" He jerked his head up to look at me.

I shook my head.

"What?" Pat asked, craning his neck to get a look at the patient.

"Nothing. Just his feathers keep getting in the way of the collar's seal," Devin lied. He eyed me with that you'd-better-know-what-you're-doing look.

"I'll take the head. You grab the legs, Dev," I ordered.

"I've got it, Amber," Pat interjected. "You don't have to stick around if ya'd rather get going."

"You just keep the gurney and inflatable in place."

"You're not actually coming with us, are you? Not on your day off?" Pat teased. "Don't you have a—"

"Not much of a choice," I said. "Section 4-7 of county protocols: Any advanced medical care provider who makes initial contact must accompany the patient to the Emergency Room."

The inexperienced medic didn't admit that he'd never heard of any such protocol, and Devin was smart enough not to comment.

We moved him on to the gurney and my suspicions had been right. Instead of weighing the thirty-five kilograms that anyone belonging to the hollow boned avian race should have, he weighed over a hundred. At our obvious strain, Pat laughed. "Getting old?"

"Shut up and drive," I snapped, rolling my eyes.

Pat actually did a good job of flying Code Three without tossing us around in the back once we were loaded and on our way. Devin did an even better job of not acting surprised when four minutes into the transport I told Pat to reduce to Code Two because our patient had regained consciousness and stabilized. He just closed his eyes and shook his head as our "critical patient" miraculously woke up on cue.

We'd talked before about how strange it was that the Hybrids had gone from being considered the heroes of our star cluster to mind raping criminals in a matter of months. We both figured someone high up had something to gain from the mass hysteria, but like with all things it would eventually pass. But from Devin's broken glass glare, he didn't appreciate being thrown into the middle of such a dangerous issue. I glared right back at him.

Our Hybrid patient interrupted our silent battle of wills. "I think it might be better if I didn't go to the hospital after all. Can you just land and let me out, please?" he asked.

Devin directed his comment to me instead of our patient. "Are you nuts, Amber? You know what kind of trouble we can get in for helping *his* kind!"

Just the week before, a doctor had lost his medical license and been sentenced to ten years of "re-education" for performing alteration surgeries on Hybrids so they could escape from Earth.

"What's going on?" Pat called from the cab.

"Nothing!" both Devin and I yelled at the same time. "Just keep your eyes forward."

"Besides," Devin persisted, "we can't just dump him in the middle of town. He needs medical attention. Let the hospital staff deal with him. We'll just put on our reports that he refused a physical exam."

It'd be the easiest and by far the safest way, I told myself. *And he really could just walk right out of the E.R.*

We both noticed our passenger was doing his best not to look out the rear window. But his eyes kept migrating that direction anyway. Following behind us was that hovercar with the Sian looking woman and child. If we had any doubts that it was his wife and child, the kid reaching out and crying when he spotted the Hybrid settled it.

Our rapidly recovering patient went through all the facial expressions of someone holding a conversation but without speaking. Through the window I watched the woman shake her head emphatically to whatever it was he was saying telepathically.

Ah hell, so much for taking the safest way.

Apparently, Devin came to the same conclusion. He slapped his forehead. After a frustrated groan, he called, "Pat, take us down and park it."

# # #

Two weeks later, after having to endure a lecture from my stupid-visor for allowing a critical patient, under arrest, to just walk away, I returned home. My only thought was of sleep. I'd waited day after day to be arrested for assisting the Hybrid, but no one had figured it out. I trudged up the front steps ready to sleep off a long shift as well as the insomnia of worry. A small holo-cube sat by my front door. I picked it up and ignited it.

The 3D image appeared, showing my patient and his family at the Towers of Melore. They had made it to the only planet within the star cluster where being Hybrids wasn't a crime.

"Who's that?" my nephew asked as he and his mom stopped by on their way to school.

"Just a grateful patient," I said, patting him on the head.

O Tannenbaum

PATRICIA DOYNE - FREMONT AREA WRITERS

The trees in the lot on Foothill were priced from $75 to $100. One noble fir sported a price tag of $185. Ridiculous! This year, we would celebrate Christmas without a tree.

Four days before Christmas when I told our youngest son no tree, he said, "Oh," and shrugged his shoulders.

The next day, he said he was going for a walk. He strode off, a lumpy backpack over one shoulder. After the accident that kept him off his feet for months, he was walking decisively.

I kept on sorting clutter into boxes—for the library, for the thrift shop, for the trash.

When he returned, he stated quietly, "We've got a Christmas tree."

"No," I said, "No tree this year."

"Yes," he said. "I just cut one for us." He regarded me steadily.

"Where on earth did you find a tree?"

"In a neighbor's yard."

"Does the neighbor know about this?"

"Of course," he said, finger-combing his shaggy, brown beard. Needles fell out. "I've been telling them they need to get rid of this tree. It's next to their retaining wall, and the roots were going to be a problem."

"So you went out and cut down their tree."

"Yup." He swiped his buzz-cut hair and dislodged a few more needles.

"What does this tree look like?"

"You know those trees we planted in the back yard, and had to take out because they were too close to the house, and growing like crazy?"

"A Monterey Pine? You cut down a Monterey Pine? For our Christmas tree?"

The answer was a big grin. "I had a folding saw in my backpack."

So he and I drove to this neighbor's yard. The pine on the lawn was enormous.

Even with the van's seats removed, it wouldn't fit. My son gritted his teeth and shoved as much as possible into the van. He brushed needles off of his black Pliny the Elder T-shirt and left the back door raised up.

"So it sticks out," he said. "It'll be okay."

"Thanks for getting rid of that old tree," said the neighbor.

"It's our Christmas tree," said my son proudly.

The neighbor turned and looked at the tree wagging behind the van like a bushy green tail, and said, "Inside your house?"

We brought tree home, left it in the front yard, and made a quick trip to the mall for last-minute errands. When we returned, my husband had removed all the branches from the lower 4' of the trunk. One more cut, and the tree was ready for the stand which looked like a thimble on the tip of a woody finger.

Once inside, the tree brushed the ceiling, 8' tall and 6' wide in spots.

"See?" my son said, "We've got a Christmas tree."

"Well," I admitted, "It certainly is fresh."

Strings of lights domesticated this jolly green giant, and between branches to fill in gaps we hung ornaments: flour-and-salt shapes that we'd rolled out, baked, and painted when the kids were toddlers; a plaster frame displaying my youngest son's pre-school face; a faded-red paper apple opening to show my middle son's second grade photo and wobbly printing; a miniature brass trombone hearkening back to my oldest's high school jazz band; a sloop from pre-kid sailing days; a beaded star from a women's coop outside Nairobi; and a wire bicycle from a booth in front of the Xian Warriors' excavation. The end product was impressive. A statement tree.

On Christmas Eve, my oldest son looked the tree over and pronounced, "It's different, but it works." My youngest, the lumberjack, just nodded and smiled.

This was our grandson's first Christmas tree. It looms behind him in photographs. Big. Bushy. A gift from my out-of-work son to the whole family. A win-win situation for everyone.

A tree that is becoming a family legend.

Slathered in Mayonnaise
KATHI HIATT - NORTH STATE WRITERS

"Oh no, the alarm didn't go off," I said, throwing the covers back and jumping out of bed. "Stupid piece-a-crap clock." A hazy recollection of hitting the snooze button did nothing to deter my continued verbal assault on the innocent timepiece.

I made a quick trip to the bathroom and slipped into the white ruffled blouse and pleated skirt I'd taken great pains to put together the night before. The skirt's matching cardigan would have to wait for cooler weather.

"Dang, dang, dang," I told my mirrored reflection. It was 1962 and my first day of high school. My plan was to keep a low profile, so the last thing I wanted was to make a spectacle of myself by walking in late for freshman orientation. With no time for the bouffant flip I'd planned, I tied my thick locks into a ponytail and descended the stairs two at a time.

"Would you like a waffle this morning, honey?" Mother asked.

"I don't have time," I said, irritated that she had offered me a waffle when it was obvious, I was running late. I shut the front door behind me with more force than necessary. Somewhere in my teenage brain, my mother and the piece-a-crap clock were to blame for my having overslept.

I walked-jogged the point-five miles to school with my new three-ring binder tucked under my arm (backpacks were not yet a thing.) By the time I arrived at the gym (the only place on campus large enough to seat the freshman class in its entirety,) I was perspiring and out of breath, and a hairline sweat had put a weird-looking kink in my carefully trimmed bangs. My one consolation was that I'd made it to orientation five minutes before the last bell rang, which gave me enough time to reserve a good spot in the center of the bleachers for myself and my best friend, Linda.

Mr. Wilcox, the school principal, greeted our first-year class with a lame knock-knock joke on a staticky sound system. After taking his cue from the feigned laughter of the up-and-coming suck-ups, he began his poster-board presentation on the consequences of ignoring school rules. It was in the middle of his warning about public displays of affection that my stomach decided to protest my refusal of Mother's waffle—loudly. I was thankful I'd already read the freshman handbook from front to back twice, because once the rumbling started I didn't hear one word Mr. Wilcox said. Instead, I spent the entire morning trying to cover up the embarrassing noises my midsection was making by squirming first one way—then the other: yawning, coughing, stretching, and everyone's personal favorite, throat clearing. The later the morning got, the louder my stomach got. The smothered giggles around me let me know how my efforts to muffle my turbulent abdomen were anything but successful.

By the time both hands came together at the top of the gym's metal-caged clock, I was sympathizing with those starving Chinese children my father alluded to whenever I complained about something Mother made for dinner.

As expected, the school cafeteria was packed with excited students sporting summer tans and greeting each other with first-day-of-school hugs and back slaps (high-fives were also not yet a thing.) Though starvation may have been my driving force at the time, Linda and I had been looking forward to having lunch in the cafeteria all summer. It was one of the few places on campus where we could check out all the cute boys in one place. And, as an added bonus, my favorite was on the menu: cheeseburgers and fries.

We each selected a plastic tray from a nearby table and joined the line behind a bitch'n (really hot) Hispanic boy with thick, curly hair and dark, velvety eyes. When the tantalizing odors of juicy cheeseburgers and crisp fries ignited another round of rolling grumbles, I silently cursed the flush I felt crawling up my face. Unsure whether or not Velvety-Eyes had heard my unruly digestive system, I sucked in my midsection, looked up at him, and smiled. He smiled back and winked—leaving me still unsure.

I paid the cashier, and with food tray in hand, scouted the cafeteria for condiments. Several students were clustered around a table in the center of the room. There they were helping themselves to mayo, mustard, ketchup, and a selection of fresh veggies. Unable to reach the condiment choices through the throngs of students gathered in front of the table, I decided to circle around to the back where there was less thronging. With one eye on my cherry cola and the other on the trays of juicy tomatoes and crisp onion slices, I failed to notice the hamburger bun that had fallen off someone's tray, slid across the floor upside down, and left a foot-long skid mark of smeared mayonnaise—until I stepped in it.

When the bun, the trail of mayo, and the recently buffed linoleum came into contact with the minimal grip on the soles of my new flats, my limbs lost control and took on a life of their own. My long, skinny legs bowed, and my feet began to slide sideways—in opposite directions. A slow stinging burn crawled up the inside of my stretched thighs. A sticky dampness soaked the armpits of my ruffled blouse. My heart began to race as an alarming and terrifying loss of self-control consumed my body. I sucked in a deep breath and, with a burst of panic-driven adrenaline, used every ounce of my strength to force my legs back together with a quick snap. This maneuver resulted in my doing a fifteen-second rigorous skate that would have bettered the fastest mode on any treadmill.

Desperate to bring my chaotic situation to a halt, I locked my knees, hoping it would give me the leverage I needed to force my feet back together. I let out a loud yelp when my ankles collided and left me with what I knew would be ugly bruises. Still gripping my tray, I foolishly thought (for a brief second) I had myself under control. But, much to my horror, I barely had enough time to heave a sigh of relief before my right foot began to slide backward and my left foot forward. I was about to do the splits—for the first time ever! The ten pints of blood that make up the human body shot to my cheeks, likening my fair complexion to a red Caribbean Habanero pepper. Torrents of sweat rolled down the sides of my face. Images of ripped tendons and the inside of an emergency room popped into my head, but every time I managed to get one foot under control, the other foot would slide in the opposite direction. I could hear someone matching each of my slip and slides with a high-pitched, "whoa," followed by an even higher-pitched, "oh shit." Leaving me no doubt that my humiliating slip and slide had drawn the unwanted attention of my peers.

Frantic and bordering on frenzied hysteria, I silently begged for a higher power to strike me dead. When that didn't happen, I sucked in a second deep breath, and with a tight grasp on my tray, tried once more to regain control of my floundering body by snapping my feet back together. This time, the maneuver sent me sailplaning in a backward circle—my elbows flapping wildly against my sides. It was then that I realized "the someone" matching each of my slips and slides with a "whoa" and an "oh shit" was me.

I'm still unsure if my feet finally came in contact with a dry portion of the linoleum, or if I simply wiped up the smeared trail of oily mayo with the bottom of my flats, but I did (somehow) finally manage to get myself under control. The mayo-slathered bun was nowhere to be seen—I'm guessing my chaotic struggle sent it flying into the abyss, And how I was able to keep my burger, fries, and sloshing cola from flying off the tray remains a mystery to this day.

Afraid the whole ordeal might be repeated if the soles of my flats lost their connection with the floor, I slowly shuffled towards the nearest dining table—still maintaining a death grip on my tray—and sat down.

Awestruck by the bizarre spectacle I had made of myself, the once noisy cafeteria was now reduced to a stunned silence. A shockwave of wide-eyed students stared at me, their faces frozen, their mouths hanging open.

Mortified and fighting back tears of agonizing embarrassment, I knew I had one of two options: break down in hysterical tears and hope my fellow students would shower me with compassion and sympathetic hugs, or feign a sense of humor by pretending I'd found my degrading ordeal amusing. Either way, my plan to keep a low profile had slipped away (literally.)

I chose the latter.

With my head held high, I shrugged my shoulders, flashed a parade-worthy smile that said *shit happens*, raised what was left of my cherry cola in a mock toast, and took a large bite of my condiment-free cheeseburger.

The shock and astonishment on the faces of my peers melted into hysterical laughter, loud applause, and even louder "whooping." Lastly (and much to my relief), my "mayonnaise-skate" performance received a standing ovation.

Smashing Attire

STEPHANIE DENMAN - MT. DIABLO

Midnight-colored Wolford stockings (that cost 100 francs—more than a café lunch with coffee) are finally going to make their debut. François, my first French quasi-boyfriend since moving to Paris, called me an hour ago and invited me over. He sounded relaxed which meant he might invite me to stay for longer than my customary Perrier. I accepted before he could finish his sentence.

"Brilliant," he said with the British clip he'd learned by studying English in England. "See you around seven."

I'd invested in quality lingerie after my first weekend away with François. "Why do you wear different colored tops and bottoms? Nothing matches," he'd commented after seeing me in my gray and white Calvin Kleins for the first time. "Is that an American habit?"

My main concerns had always been that my underwear was clean and wasn't the white, shapeless briefs my mother wore. Evidently, I'd needed to expand my repertoire.

Glancing at the clock, I switch on the radio and hear the song "The King of Wishful Thinking" – playing as usual. The movie *Pretty Woman* has made the single a hit this year. How appropriate. I feel like Julia Roberts' character – unpolished – not a prostitute. Sitting on my futon mattress to open the fancy black and white Wolford envelope, I open the package and slather my hands with Nivea lotion before extracting the hose. The legs are stacked neatly on top of each other as if I'd caught them spooning. I turn the package to see if there are directions. There aren't. Until now, I'd never felt the need to invest in any hose I couldn't find at the drugstore. But attracting François had rebuilt my self-esteem and keeping him intrigued had become an obsession, particularly since my American fiancé had dumped me within months of our arrival in France to chase runway models.

Shaking one leg out to its full length, I point my foot into the non-reinforced toe and carefully guide the stocking in stages up my leg. It feels silky and naughty.

Repeating the ritual with the other leg, I slip on a black mini dress, spray the air with Jean Paul Gaultier Eau de Toilette and walk through the perfume cloud. Six-fifty already and it's going to take me at least fifteen minutes to get to François' place. Timing is tricky because it's gauche to be punctual in Paris, but François gets irritated if I'm more than ten minutes late. Outside my fourth-floor apartment, I grip the stairway rail and negotiate three flights of perpetually polished and as-slippery-as-an-ice-rink-after-a-Zamboni stairs, step-by-step, in my kitten heels. While heaving open the building's lacquered, green front door, I feel slippage. Propping the door open with my left hip, I adjust my right stocking through my dress and then the left. The concierge steps out of her loge just in time to witness me straddling the entrance. She watches me, shakes her head, muttering, and goes back inside where I'm sure she sits spying behind her curtain.

Five minutes to six already, so I keep moving and step out into the mild September evening. Swallows swoop by en route to the *Eglise Saint Eustache* where they'll roost until the sun sets. It feels like a scene from *Snow White*, which inspires me to skip for a few steps – until the stockings slip again.

There are a few ways to get to François' apartment on rue Réaumur from mine on Pierre Lescot. Given the time, I choose the short-cut down rue Saint-Denis, the Paris equivalent of Amsterdam's Red-Light District. Prostitutes some in pairs, some alone pose in doorways in lace, Spandex, and stilettos. At the top of the first block, I pull up one of the stockings which has slipped to just under the hem of my dress and take a deep breath.

Most streets in Paris are swept regularly by men with long brooms with green plastic fronds or sprayed by a street sweeper. But rue Saint-Denis has been neglected. Half-eaten kabobs, tiny wax paper squares that wrapped baguettes, cigarette butts, Durex condom wrappers, and the ubiquitous dog poop blanket the macadam and gutters, detritus from nights and days of hunting, preying, and carousing. Unlike other Paris streets, there's no scaffolding erected here to clean the ancient buildings. These old dames, some of them formerly magnificent *Hôtel Particuliers*, are left to decay, growing dingier with time.

Marching ahead, I take two paces, stop, and move into an empty entry to adjust again in semi-private. Back on the *rue*, a prostitute observes me, takes a drag of her cigarette, and arches an eyebrow. "*Bonsoir,*" I mouth, look down quickly, and walk a bit further. Both stockings slide to my knees. Snickering ladies of the night elbow each other, watching my painful progression. I glance at two women three doors down and they just stare.

How do Victoria's Secret models make this look so easy? Why choose now, of all times, to ditch your pantyhose to try something new?

Sweating, though it's chilly, I think back to our first date a month ago. François was the office catch, a high-potential professional at the software company where I was working as a reference writer. Barrel chested, compact, and well-dressed he resembled a fashionable Napoleon. After flirting with him around the coffee maker a few times, he'd asked me to lunch.

"Um ... um ... yes, *oui*. Sure," I'd said, looking around the office kitchen to verify that he was talking to me. It turned out we lived in the same neighborhood so we'd agreed to meet that Saturday at a local restaurant, *35 dans l'ombre*, 35 degrees (Celsius) in the shade.

That Saturday was sweltering coincidentally, but I'd asked the waiter if we could sit outside anyway. The waiter looked at François for affirmation.

"It's so nice to see the sun for a change," I'd explained. Paris was gray, not "*gay Paree.*" François hesitated, raised his eyebrows at the waiter, and then smiled, "Why not?"

Wearing a navy-blue blazer with a navy-blue sweater draped in a calculated, jaunty position around his shoulders, and pressed beige slacks, François stood until I sat down. I felt sweat collecting above my lip, but his face was smooth and dry. His extra dousing of Fahrenheit 451 helped mask the smell of frying urine from the dogs and drunks who frequented this neighborhood at night.

"I'm glad you finally worked up the courage to take me out," I'd teased after we ordered. So many women at work would've died to lunch with him.

"It was nothing," he'd said. *Nothing? Meaning it didn't take courage or does this mean nothing?*

"My last girlfriend, Adriana, was Romanian," François started.

Last girlfriend? Was I his new girlfriend by going out to lunch with him? Are we a thing? What a strange way to start a conversation.

"She had dark hair and wore a tiny tail in the back." He'd turned his head to show where her pigtail would've sprouted and giggled.

I ran my hand through my hair. *Is my hair kookie enough? Am I provocative? Maybe I should wear it up next time.*

"And you know, one day, she got her hair cut. Snipped it right off. I was so disappointed. Too bad. I liked that little tail." He'd shrugged to himself. "She had a *mariage blanc*, how do you say... a marriage of convenience...with a French man who was very big in the party scene here in Paris. Oh my God, she was sooo talented. You know, she spoke FIVE languages. She was *vraiement genial.*"

He thinks she was so great. Say something clever. "Really? I'm, uh, good at calligraphy."

"One time," he'd continued, hunching and leaning forward as if he was about to tell me some juicy gossip, "She actually tried to cheat me and my buddy out of 2500 francs each!" His eyes were starry.

Five hundred dollars was certainly chutzpa.

"She told us this story about how her mother was desperately sick in Romania and how she had to get back to see her before it was too late. And could we loan her the money?" He threw his head back and laughed remembering. "She was so street smart. Can you imagine the audacity?"

I can't imagine because I would never think to cheat someone. Okay, I might pocket a ten-dollar bill if I found one on the street, but I wouldn't hatch an elaborate plan. What the heck was so special about her? "She sounds fascinating," I'd said.

He droned on about Adriana, giving me a chance to examine him. He was handsome with dark, wavy brown hair and thin 60's style sideburns. His aquiline nose was characteristic of French men, and though it looked like the mast of a schooner, it worked on him. His skin was tanned, probably from tennis and not a salon, and when he smiled, I could see his exaggerated, pointy canines.

It looks like his bite would be worse than his bark.

"Can you believe it?" he'd asked.

No, I shook my head. *What did he just say? I thought he'd be more imaginative than this. And more interested in me. Why is Miss Romania so amazing?* I stifled a yawn and was relieved when our food arrived. But his enormous *Salade de Chevre Chaud* didn't stop him from rattling on about Adriana's adventures.

There's nothing in this little bonsai man for me. As he waxed on, I continued my visual voyage anyway of the parts of his body exposed above the table. Tiptoeing down the sleeve of his polyester blazer with my eyes, I saw one of his cufflinks peeking out from under his sleeve. It had an asterisk and an exclamation point. To me, it screamed whimsy or humor possibly. I was hopeful. A sense of humor packaged with his looks. I'd decided not to dismiss this guy so quickly. I would become as exotic as Adriana.

I'd worked hard to be arresting this last month since that first date. Back on the rue St. Denis, I flex my thighs and try walking knock-kneed, hoping the tension and controlled movement will keep these hose from hell in place.

The end of the block is still five buildings and fifteen prostitutes away. A few more steps and I forget and relax my thighs. One stocking flutters to my knee. I hitch it up and notice a hooker wearing hot pants with stockings secured in place with a garter belt. *Garter belt. Just like mom wore in the '60s. Totally forgot. Too late now.* Plotting my next move, I scrunch the sides of my skirt, working my fingers until I feel the tops of my stockings. I pinch my skirt and stockings together like chopsticks and drag one leg behind me, like Igor inching to my destination.

At last, I arrive at the corner and turn left. A pharmacy, a Franprix mini-mart, and a real estate office line the home stretch to François' apartment. *Who knows if he'll even appreciate this? Remember when you tried to assimilate by sunbathing topless? He told you to put on your top.*

It's been a strange relationship but the only steady one I've had since breaking up with my fiancé, another man on the fast track and the reason I was in Paris to begin with. It had been a hard two years since he broke things off. I'd started over again as a grad student at the American School of Paris, got working papers, and had finally caught the eye of a sought-after bachelor. François is intelligent, funny, and drives a car – a real perk in Paris. But he's like dating a cat. Everything is on his terms. If he wants affection, he'll come to me. But if I want a cuddle, or reassurance, he's prickly and standoffish. Date a catlike man or end up a spinster with a cat? The choice is clear for now.

It's the first step down the last leg of this damned voyage. My hands are cramping and as I unfurl them, both stockings drift down. I'm exhausted. Just two doors away from François' place I stop to look at my reflection in the shop window. My Wolford's are welled around my ankles. The shop sign says *Fermé*. Looking around, I see no one, so I bend over and hitch the bastard stockings up to my underwear, lifting my skirt in the process to clear the way. *This is nuts.* Richard Gere ultimately fell for Julia Roberts because she was natural. Blowing out my breath, I shove the stockings down, step out of my heels, remove, ball up, and stuff the stockings into my purse.

BANG! A car smashes into another. *I hope that crash was because of me.*

The Hungry After

SHERIDA BUSH - MT. DIABLO

Night came early that day. Lena's footsteps echoed on the sidewalk as darkness enveloped the small downtown. Only a few street lights lit a dim path. Lena pulled her coat tighter as she walked past the abandoned windows of the stores. Even Santa's house in the town center, glowing with colored lights on most Christmas Eves, was dark and deserted.

Two men walked toward her on the opposite side of the street. She tensed, paused, and watched them. Earlier in the month, three men had assaulted her and grabbed her purse. She had just finished replacing her credit cards, license, phone, and door locks. Lena's shoulders relaxed when they passed by.

An older man sat propped up against a wall wearing an elf hat. He was asleep, or passed out. A sign on his lap read, "Santa's Helper Needs Help. Please." She put a couple of dollars in his empty tin. That was all of the money she had on her, except for what she needed to buy a sandwich at the corner store.

"Hi, Sam," she said as she entered.

"Hey, girl. I put a turkey and cheese aside for you. Bon appétit." Sam often kept a day-old sandwich to the side for her at half price. "Any job news?"

"No, but today's interview went pretty well. I think. The bus had no heat again, and I'm frozen. Uh, I keep forgetting to tell you that Megan moved out. You know she's been in a bad way since her fiancée died. She ran out of money, so she had to move in with her mom."

"She went back to Minnesota? Damn."

"I know. Two feet of snow this week. She was a good friend, not just a roommate, and I miss her. How's business?"

"Bad, but we're hanging on. Wish they'd keep the bleepin' electricity on. We can't stay open long on a generator." Lena just then noticed the store was almost as dim as the street. But Sam's wide smile underscored by his neat black beard made her feel better. He wore a Santa hat.

"Saw Earl on the street," said Lena. "Sleeping or whatever. Hope he's OK."

"I'll check on him later. There's a new soup kitchen where the church on Elm used to be. They let him sleep in a room in the back on cold nights. I'll see if I can get him in there."

"Soup kitchen? Who runs it?"

"A guy who led some kind of big nonprofit before the outbreak hit. Mike. He saw a lot of people going hungry in town and wrangled some public and private money for it. He calls it Open Door."

"Sounds cool. Well, goodnight and thanks. Stay safe."

"Lena," Sam said as she reached the door, "we're leaving tomorrow with the kids to visit Marina's family. The store will be closed for a few days. Will you be . . . "

Lena turned to face him. "I'll be OK. Really."

Sam did not look convinced. "Hey, we won't be selling these, so just take them." Sam loaded three more sandwiches into her bag. "How . . . without a roommate, rent will be tough, right?"

"Next month will be fine, then we'll see." Lena straightened her posture and lifted her head. "You enjoy time with your family and thank you so much for the sandwiches." Lena left smiling, and yelled from outside: "I'm happy that you're finally getting some time off."

The deserted streets were quiet but for her slow footfalls. The thought of a place, any place, with signs of life drew her to the new charity. Her once-cramped apartment was now spare and lifeless post-Meghan. Going home this night meant cold, dim solitude.

Against the gloom of the night, the leaded glass windows of Open Door invited with a golden, flickering light. The warmth inside fogged the panes. "Wow," she said out loud. She hesitated, paced a moment then strode forward. Opening the door, she was astonished to hear a holiday tune played on a violin. A real, live violin, not a recording. She'd heard live music only once in many months—a lone bagpiper at a funeral.

Candles, oil lamps, and battery-powered lanterns gave a soft glow to the cavernous room. Thirty or so people sat clustered at long tables, talking in low voices or listening to the music. Lena waved at a couple she knew who had owned a downtown store, now closed. Enthralled with the violinist, they didn't see her. A huge Christmas tree stood in stark outline against the wall on her left like a furry spider. On the opposite wall, a cafeteria-style row of steam tables and waiting food stretched down the long room.

A man on the food line beckoned her in with the aluminum tongs in his hand. She approached shaking her head, "I'm not going to eat here. I can eat at home. I . . . "

"Everyone is welcome here," he said. His eyes shone in the candlelight. "You can have a banquet at home, but if you're eating it alone, it's thin gruel indeed."

She stared at him with her mouth open, not sure what to say. Aromas of turkey and stuffing enticed her. "I, well . . . it does smell wonderful. Are you Mike?" Lena thought he might be in his early 60s. The man nodded.

"One of them. Mike Senior at your service. My son, Mike Junior, runs the place, and his sister is the one playing the violin. She's Mikeala." He waited for a reaction and wasn't disappointed. "I know—my wife had a fixation on my name. I could never deny her anything."

"She's a lucky woman."

"She isn't with us anymore. It . . . you know . . . took her almost two years ago."

"I'm so sorry." Lena closed her eyes as the faces of those she had lost appeared unbidden in her mind. When she opened them, Mike had turned away, then cleared his throat as he turned back.

"Thank you. How about some chow? Tonight, we have tasty roast turkey and stuffing, mashed potatoes—the works. It's pretty good if I say so myself. And served with a smile." He clacked his tongs like castanets.

"How can I resist?" Lena's empty, grouchy stomach convinced her to stay. Mike Senior loaded her plate with food and called to a man seated up front, Mike Junior.

The younger Mike beckoned her to sit across from him as his sister finished playing "We Wish You a Merry Christmas," and disappeared into the kitchen. Lena and Mike exchanged introductions as he studied her face.

"Do you live around here? You look familiar."

"Yes, just about three blocks away." Lena tasted a mouthful of stuffing, and it took her back to past holidays at home. "This is delicious."

"Thanks. My recipe." His kind manner dissolved her uneasiness as they talked about their lives before the world stopped and their lives after. He looked conspiratorial when he leaned in and said, "It only occurred to me what Open Door's initials stood for after I opened the place. It was too late to change it, so I say we OD on good feelings here."

Lena groaned. "Geez, corny. How many people do you get here?"

"Maybe 100 a day. We're open for fourteen hours every day, but we're not well known yet. A lot of people are embarrassed, like it's a shameful thing to come here. We're trying to lose the soup kitchen reputation and be thought of as a community center, a gathering place."

"Changing an image is difficult. I ran into that a lot as an event planner and doing public relations."

Mike sat up. "We could use some volunteer help. Everything from cooking, serving, cleanup to . . . to changing our image." Lena knew that was coming, but she didn't mind. She liked the idea of coming here.

"If I get a job, I probably won't have much free time. But I can do a little something now."

"You mean *when* you get a job. In the meantime, can you come by tomorrow afternoon? That's a good time to talk." His smile drooped. "Oh, it's Christmas day tomorrow, so you're probably busy."

"It's all right. I can be here."

"Great. Stay for the party in the evening; there'll be more live music and of course a visit from Santa." Mike tilted his head toward his dad.

As the last word left his mouth, a burst of colored Christmas lights flooded the room from every wall. The dark, sprawling Christmas tree transformed from a giant spider to a sparkling jewel of white lights. The tune "Jingle Bells" filled the air. Lena looked at Mike, and they both laughed. "Guess the power's on," she said.

". . . Jingle all the way . . . ," rang out as all sang in tuneful chaos. Lena felt something she had long lost. Mike looked straight in her eyes.

"Tomorrow will be a good day," he said over the din.

Lena nodded. "Agreed."

The Journey
ALICIAGAEL - COASTAL DUNES

CHAPTER 1
County Sligo, Ireland
June 1832

"Through this holy anointing, may the Lord in his love and mercy help you with the grace of the Holy Spirit. May the Lord who frees you from sin save you and raise you up." **Tommy's** uncle Liam, a Catholic Priest, finished reciting the Holy Sacrament of Last Rights, walked to the wooden crucifix that hung in the far corner of the cottage, took out his mahogany beads, and began praying the Rosary.

Tommy's eight-year-old sister, Annie, lay on the floor near the hearth, sobbing. His mother sat on the edge of the bed holding his father's limp hand, silently praying. His father lay dying on the bed. It had been less than a week since his father had stepped on a rusty nail, piercing the paper-thin sole of his boot. The resulting infection had spread quickly throughout his body, and he had been in and out of consciousness with fever for the past two days. His breathing had become shallow and weak in the last hour. There was nothing they could do to save him. It was only a matter of time.

Tommy knelt on the opposite side of the bed. His hands clasped together, his eyes squeezed shut. He prayed, begged, and promised to dedicate his life to the church if only God wouldn't take his father. He opened his eyes; his father was looking at him, trying to speak. Tommy leaned in and placed his head next to his father's.

"Promise me you'll take care of yer mam and sister," his father whispered.

Tears streamed down Tommy's face. "No, Da. I'm not a man yet. Please don't go. Please, Da, don't go."

His father closed his eyes. "Promise me, Tommy."

Tommy grabbed his father's hand and held it to his face. "I promise, Da. I promise ta look after them." His voice choked with pain.

His father opened his eyes one last time and looked at Tommy. "Make me proud, son." After that, his chest didn't rise again.

"No, Da. No," Tommy begged.

He watched his mother reach out and close his father's eyelids, then she leaned over and kissed him on the lips. Annie rushed over and threw herself on top of her father, begging God to bring him back. Father Liam walked over, picked up Annie, and cradled her in his arms.

"There, there, girl. He is with God now. He's looking down on us; he'll watch over you. He'll always be with you." Father Liam held Annie to his chest. Tommy saw a tear run down his uncle's cheek.

###

"Promise me you'll take care of yer mam and sister." His father's dying words played over and over in his head as he stood at the edge of the rocky shore. The promise weighed heavily on his thirteen-year-old shoulders.

He stood there, watching a sizeable wooden ship cross the horizon. The cold mist knifed into his skin; his thin frame trembled against the icy wind that howled off the Atlantic Ocean. He ignored the discomfort, just like he ignored the lone seagull that screamed overhead; he steadied his gaze on the ship.

Workers on the waterfront took little notice of the coatless boy. Times were brutal on the island; few Irish families had money for anything other than necessities, and many went without. Death was always near; like a menacing shadow, it lurked in the back of the room and patiently waited its turn.

A gust of wind blew his father's green tweed cap, two sizes too big, over eyes the same shade of gray as the turbulent ocean waters. The same eyes as his father's. A single tear slid down his cheek but dried quickly in the harsh wind. He missed his father. His death had left him angry: at his father for dying and leaving them penniless, at his inability to find work, and furious at the English for turning a blind eye as the Irish starved.

The ship on the horizon slowly grew larger as it headed toward the port. Tommy didn't know how he would make it happen, but someday a ship like that would take him away from the hell Ireland had become.

Annie ran up and took his hand. Her red hair blew wild in the wind, and she shivered in the cold; the thin coat she wore was at least a size too small.

"That's a big boat, Tommy." She smiled up at him.

He squeezed her hand. "That's the *Josephine*. And it's a packet ship, not a boat." His eyes never left the horizon.

"Come on, Tommy." She tugged his hand, trying to pull him away. "Mam's waiting for us. It'll be dark soon."

He pulled his gaze from the ship and smiled at her, squeezing her hand again. "You're right, Annie, we don't want Mam ta worry about us. She has enough ta worry about."

After one last look at the ship, now close enough to see the crew bustling about the deck, they turned and began their walk down the long dirt road toward home.

The one-lane path was narrow, just wide enough for a single wagon. If wagons coming from different directions met, the one going uphill would have to back up until there was room for the other to go around. Before their father's death, they would have ridden in the family's pony cart, pulled by Dougie, the donkey his father had brought home years ago in a trade with his second cousin Paddy for a gallon of homemade poteen. But with no means to support themselves, they'd sold the cart and Dougie to put food on the table.

The village they lived in was small, barely a dot on the map. Located on the west side of the island, the weather was harsh. The rocky terrain wasn't fit for farming much of anything. The best land was occupied by absent English landowners who raised cattle. The Irish, forbidden from owning land in their own country, had no choice but to rent small plots from the English occupiers.

The road to the village was dotted with small, two-room thatched-roof cottages, most abandoned, their straw roofs falling in. Those that remained looked as depressed and disheartened as the people inside. The population now numbered less than a dozen families. For generations, the Golden clan had grown potatoes and raised sheep in the rocky countryside overlooking Sligo Bay. The potato failure of 1830 forced many to leave for Galway or Dublin, hoping to find work in the cities. Tommy remembered his friend Erin O'Malley. Erin's father had taken the family to Dublin, hoping to find work. Since they'd left a year ago, there'd been no word from them.

Tommy looked down at Annie, who silently skipped beside him. "I wasn't able to find work, Annie."

"Tommy, there isn't any work for anyone," she said, pulling red curls away from her face, the wind making it impossible to control them.

"I'm afraid we'll be going without supper again tonight." A sob caught in his throat. "I'm sorry, Annie." He looked away, not wanting her to see the tears in his eyes.

"Don't worry, Tommy, Mam says God will provide, and I believe her." She looked up at him and grinned. Her innocence broke his heart.

"I wish I had your faith, Annie. Right now, I feel like God's abandoned us."

"No, Tommy, he hasn't. He's testing us," she said in all seriousness as they approached their own small dwelling. The heat from the peat burning in the fireplace warmed them when they entered.

"It's about time you two returned," said their mother, who sat in front of the fire, sipping tea with Father Liam.

"Father Liam brought us potatoes from Boyle." She continued. "We'll eat good tonight for sure." The smile on her face didn't reach her eyes. "He also brought news from your aunt in America," she said as Annie climbed onto her mother's lap and Tommy found a place by the fire.

Father Liam took a sip of tea from a chipped gray mug, then cleared his throat. "I'm sure yer father told you about our sister, Ester. She married an American visitor then moved with him to New York. It's been a dozen or so years she's been gone now."

He looked from one child to the other. "Annie, you weren't even born yet, and Tommy, you were still in nappies when she left."

"Father told us about her, but I don't remember her or the man she married," Tommy said, returning his hands to the warmth of the fire.

"His name was Michael O'Donnell. He's a nephew of Daniel O'Donnell." Father Liam pointed to the wall where a picture of Daniel O'Donnell, the Catholic Association leader who advocated for Irish Catholics' rights, hung. Nearly every Catholic family in Ireland had a similar portrait of O'Donnell in their home. "Michael's parents were from County Kerry. He was in County Sligo visiting his kin. Ester was quite taken with him and didn't hesitate ta marry and leave Ireland. She always loved an adventure." He smiled and let out a small chuckle, then his face became serious. "I wrote ta her about your father's passing. She was devastated by the news. Hugh was special ta her. He was the youngest of us, only two years old when our mother passed. Ester took it upon herself ta take care of him, even though she was only eight." Father Liam took out a well-worn handkerchief and wiped tears from his eyes before continuing. "She sent her condolences and an offer."

Tommy glanced at his mother. A tear ran down her cheek, which she quickly wiped away.

Father Liam took another sip from his mug then continued. "Tommy, she wants ya to go to America. She and her husband will pay for the voyage, and yer'll live with them until ya can make yer own way."

Tommy stared at his uncle, unsure what to say. His mind raced. Going to America was his dream, but how could he leave his mother and sister? How would they get by without him?

Would he ever see them again? He'd promised his father he'd provide for them. Would his father want him to go?

"I know yer worried about leaving yer mam and sister," Father Liam said.

Tommy wondered if Catholic priests could read minds.

"I've talked to the widow Chamberlain. She's a Protestant but a good Christian woman all the same. She would be open to yer mother and sister moving into her home in exchange for cooking and cleaning. Her health has declined since her husband died, and she's getting on in years. The house is too big for her to take care of, and she doesn't want to move to London to live with her son. It's a fair arrangement for both. Your mam agrees."

"Tommy, I told ya God would provide." Annie grinned.

Tommy nodded and gave her a small smile, then turned back to his uncle.

Father Liam leaned forward, rested his elbows on his knees, and brought his palms together as if in prayer. Tommy's heart beat so loudly he was sure they could all hear it.

His uncle looked Tommy in the eye. "Do you want to go to America, Thomas?"

Love: A Catalogue

NANCY CAVERS DOUGHERTY - REDWOOD WRITERS

Let love reflect—
      gather the sunshine
into soft folds, a shawl to place
over your shoulders as a ray of light
glances across his brow,
the handsome silhouette refracting into multiple
associations of times past, to come,
hopes and dreams shared, collected.

A private library,
yours only; the two card holders
to these most precious
archives.

Let love collect—
      with randomness
and an abandon for every moment,
the odd mementoes;
a book of matches, piece of sea glass,
the bent serving spoon, a dog-eared menu,
what your hands and his have graced.

Let love remember—
every hurdle
and impossible detour, personal
or imposed; the wildfires, floods,
break-ins, shattered glass—
all good stand-ins for the dark corners
of soul too hard, too cold to fathom,
and merciless.

Only the clasp of hands,
yours to his, the steadying
warmth of palms
helps save and guides
to calmer shores.

Let love restore—
        by forgiveness, humbleness,
to return to this bond,
invisible maybe, but as tangible
as sun's rays are strong
as sparkly as the green of dew
upon lawn, the music of his voice
and the song of yours.

Let love embrace—
        the adventure;
here, it is yours to write,
to let your imaginations soar.

Family Tree

KAY KRATTLI - CENTRAL COAST WRITERS

Sharp on the air
   the scent of fresh tree blood. New cuts
      gleam bone white in the eucalyptus.

Below on the cool stones,
   still too alive to know they are dead,
      green branches stare at their ancestors and
         wonder at the change in perspective.

Offshoot of a twisted trunk,
   I cut myself from my family tree,
      hacked limb from root to escape.

Grieving lost certainty of place,
   I miss the tangle of limb on limb in wind,
      and the soft rustlings of leaf kin left behind.

Self-amputation without an arborist
   ensures wounds are likely,
      but my soul was already traced
         with a fine web of scars.

Alone, a mere sapling,
    autonomy holds no fear, nor does
      age mandate obedience.
         I revel in my new perspective.
         From here I can see
            survival.

The Mountain

KATHLEEN ANDERSEN - NAPA VALLEY WRITERS

"Do not go gentle into that good night. Rage, rage against the dying of the light."
Dylan Thomas, age 33

Where's Gordon? He's not behind me. I shouldn't have walked so far ahead. I'll wait for him here—

I need a rest anyway. My heart's racing and I'm so short of breath. What's the elevation of this climb? We've hiked many mountains together and stayed in good condition, but oxygen levels fall as you age and at 86 allowances must be made. Is this a glacier? I'm surrounded by snow but warm from the exertion and don't feel the cold. I should have stayed with Gordon. I worry about his heart. He should have caught up to me by now.

"Gordon! Gordon!" My call sounds so weak I doubt he'll hear me.

"Dr. Mayer." My nurse leans over and touches my shoulder. "We can't allow your husband in the ICU. It's for his safety. We wouldn't want him to get Covid."

"No, of course not. I was dreaming."

Or hallucinating. My brain is foggy. The fields of snow are really white sheets surrounding me in drifts on my bed. I crane my neck to look at the monitor. Of all the numbers and tracings, there's only one I need to see. My oxygen saturation is 83%. It was 87% this morning. I lean back into the pillow and close my eyes, wanting to forget 83. I pick at the loose sheets over me, as if they're the cause of this constriction around my chest that's making it so hard to breathe. I focus on the cool flow of supplemental oxygen on my face. It's high flow, and surely the highest rate that can be delivered short of intubation. From my days working here, I know that the team should be assembling right now to intubate me. But I've told them not to.

Yesterday when it became clear that my Covid infection was too severe to treat at home, I told Gordon as gently as I could that I wouldn't be intubated. He tried to hold me with his eyes.

"You can get through this." Then he whispered, "Don't leave me, Marian."

I took his hand in both of mine. "Please, Gordon. I'm tired. It's my time."

I was honest with him. "Two courses of chemotherapy have sapped me. Intubation would likely mean weeks on the ventilator with a tracheotomy and gastric feeding tube, and profound debility from weeks of bed confinement. Recovery, if I survive, would be too long and too hard, and I can't climb that mountain now. I'm old, and I'm tired." I didn't mention that it would also be too long and too hard for him and for Helen and Tom who have their own lives in other states.

He is capable, and he trusts me. I visualize him as a young man, when we first met in college. I was studious and so limited. He introduced me to long hikes in the mountains, and my self-reliance and perspective expanded with the exertion and the panoramic views. Gordon nurtured my confidence, and this made me a better person and physician. Whenever I tell him this, he shakes his head, denying any role in my maturation. It must please him, though.

I try to push out the pangs of regret that are creeping in–the decades of trying to be the best mother, the best doctor, the best wife, and the inevitable failure in all three. The extra work for Gordon and the discord this caused until more men joined in domestic chores. The guilt of leaving school projects and cupcakes to other mothers. I tell myself to look at Helen and Tom today. Behind closed eyes I see a kaleidoscope of their images, starting with their births and the joy that enveloped us. Whirling through my mind are views of them with tiny new teeth, then spaces where teeth should be, and the charming gawky look when adult teeth filled their smiles. Like a film on fast forward, I see their school years, our vacations, graduations, marriages, and grandchildren. The illnesses, heartbreaks, failures, and conflicts I edit and leave on the cutting room floor. A life as good as one can hope to have. Gordon, Helen, Tom. They soothe and warm me.

I'm jolted by bells and alarms. I still react to them, and am relieved when I realize it's someone else's job now. The hospital is busier—every bed is filled. So much looks foreign to me. The staff wear spacesuits, not white coats, and are faceless. Lifting, turning, assessing, reassuring—the work is relentless and they are so committed. I remember my own work.

I picture one of my patients sitting silently in a wheelchair as her family urged her to "fight," eat more, and get better and stronger. I watched her face, saw the profound fatigue, the discouragement, the guilt of disappointing loved ones by not enduring more rounds of physical therapy, chemotherapy, any therapy. She worked and struggled all her life, and suffered as all humans suffer, and wanted just to rest at the end. I'm ready for this rest.

I am ready to go gentle into that good night.

I feel so foggy. How can I still be warm surrounded by all of this snow? I have rested long enough. Time to head down the mountain. I'm sure to find Gordon. It's getting easier. Walking downhill always is. I feel colder now as I descend. We must be hiking in the Alps–

I hear village bells. They are more distorted and distant, softer... quieter.

Steeped

STEVEN LUBLINER - REDWOOD WRITERS

"Is there tea?" my dad would ask
With his best self-pitying glance.
My mom would set to the task,
And there'd be Lipton.

The problem with such moments is
Things I thought to say like
"Can't you make it yourself" or
"Can't you just ask nicely"
Failed to grasp precisely
How they got there.

I only saw the man on the couch,
In his underwear and expectations.
Not his years of deprivations. Not his fear.
So, who demanded tea?
The 12-year-old refugee.
The teenage soldier and the man grown older
On bridges and in tunnels and in airports
Lugging wheelless luggage on
Ulcer making jobs that kept us
Safe in comfort and in unremarkable tea.

I only saw the woman in the kitchen
With her head in the oven, at ease
Lighting the pilot, broiling burgers,
And timing American cheese.
She deserved at least a please.
She deserved to be let alone.
She taught me to scrape toast, sizzle bacon,
Baste an egg, and make an omelet with rubbery ham.
"The best chefs in the world are men."
By this she meant two things:
"Be better than your dad,"
And "boys are best."

In later years, I'd take her out.
The waitress would come by
With brown and orange pots and offer "Coffee?"
"Yes, *with* the meal," she'd spit.
Some depression era fear of double charging?
A remembered forties diner dance:
The coffee then the Lucky then the Chicken à la King?
Yes, *this* is how one eats out.
Before things fall apart.

"She's just doing her job," I'd say.
My mom would shake her head.
"Stupid girl," she'd say.
"Stupid girl."

The Twice-Told Tale

ELAINE DREW - TRI-VALLEY WRITERS

The men returned early from the hunt. Smoke from the fire mingled with the smell of wet wool. The air in the hall was close, the weather too fierce to open a door. As we assembled for dinner, the butler told the king and me that the bridge into town had been swept away by the surging Itchen. The musicians and the troupe of players, the evening's entertainment, would not make it tonight.

The king noticed the look on my face. "Don't give it a thought, my love," he said to me. "I will tell a story."

"In that case, Your Majesty," I said, "we'd better serve extra wine." I beckoned the steward.

We lingered over the meal—the poached fowl with bacon did not disappoint, and the broiled venison was a success—but once the honey-glazed pears had been served, dinner could no longer be extended. The steward had not neglected the wine glasses, and King Egbert rose to tell his tale. If the court anticipated a dull evening, they were smart enough to hide it.

"There was once a king who had a large hall and many loyal retainers. He had recently married a beautiful queen, not as beautiful as our queen, but close. Her hair was as fine and lustrous as silk thread. Her bosom overflowed her gown like the river that's rising above its banks tonight. Besides his fetching wife, this king had a large stable and ample grooms."

When Egbert mentioned the stable, I knew the tale he would tell. I'd heard it.

"One day, the queen called for her horse, and a young man named Anson brought it to her. As he hoisted her onto her mount, she glanced down at him. She rode off; he stared after her. His legs became wobbly, and his breath shallow and quick. The groom collapsed, conquered by the archer who sends invisible darts.

"Now this boy had some sense, and he realized that he must stifle this unsuitable passion. And for some time, he did. Or at least he refrained from acting on it. Can determination subdue desire?"

The listeners chimed in with a cacophony of opinions, and there was no clear verdict on the topic. Some thought it could, while others weren't convinced.

"In this case, the fellow's will began to desert him, and lust marched into the empty spaces. Anson concluded that, although the price be his life, he must have the woman. For weeks he studied the king's movements, skulking about at a safe distance. Anson noted the time of night that the king visited his lady in her chamber. The young man discovered that a chambermaid and a lady of the court had both caught the king's fancy, and that there were nights he did not spend in his lady's bed. Anson overheard the soft low whistle that signaled the king was at the bedchamber door. With practice the groom became adept, and the king himself could not have told their trilling apart.

"The groom discerned a pattern to the king's rotation. In time, the night arrived when Anson convinced himself he was ready. He plunged into the chilly Itchen to remove the stench of the stable. He donned the shirt he reserved for church and shadowed the king. He watched him go to a mistress. The coast was clear. Anson whistled at the queen's chamber, and her yawning maid opened the door.

"The maid was not the only one who was sleepy. The queen was quietly snoring when this lover arrived, and barely stirred during their encounter, which, with Anson's excitement, didn't last long."

There were sympathetic nods from a few of the warriors, who probably didn't last long themselves.

"This state of affairs continued, with Anson carefully choosing his moment. While his enthusiasm never waned, after their first night the stableboy could control himself well enough that the queen, now awake, was abundantly pleased. Anson's midnight forays went on for some time with no one the wiser.

"There came a night, however, when the chambermaid, weary of the king's fatuous promises to elevate her to a lady of the court, complained. They had a tiff. Annoyed, the king sought his other lover, only to find she was visiting her sister in Basingstoke. He arrived at his wife's door shortly after Anson had departed.

"He got into bed beside his wife who said, 'My lord, you are amorous tonight.' Hearing this, the king felt a little guilty and wondered what she knew about his escapades. 'I am always amorous when you are near,' he tried.

"'Indeed, sir, you are no slouch. But having so vigorously attended me earlier, I didn't expect to see you again tonight.'

"The king knew he had done no such thing." Our storyteller paused, milking the moment. Then he addressed the hall: "What do you think he did?"

"He killed her on the spot," bellowed one of the men. Most heads nodded in agreement, except for the cautious, who didn't want to chance being wrong. They were biding their time to see which way the tale would turn.

"That's not what he did," said Egbert.

Several voices shouted out: "He chided her severely!"

"He whipped her soundly!"

"Ran from the room in pursuit of her lover!"

"Cut off her nose!"

"No, no, no, and certainly not!" said Egbert. "The king could see the lady had been tricked and was guiltless. He saw no need to shame her or distress her with painful information. Besides, if this fellow was such a skillful lover and had filled in on the nights the king had been off dallying, His Majesty figured he might as well take the credit. So he made love to his wife, rather quickly, because he had a pressing mission.

"The king was an experienced chieftain used to thinking on his feet. He swiftly formulated a plan. He would go through his hall and inspect the warriors where they slept. A pounding heart or labored breathing would betray his man. As the king left the bedchamber, he tripped over his hastily tossed boot and, when he fell, a piece of straw jabbed his face. He adjusted his plan and started with the stable.

"The groomsmen lay in the hay, snoring with admirable invention—all except one, who had just turned in and was replaying the night's amorous adventures. Anson heard someone enter the stable, and his pricking conscience feared it might be the king. His heart beat like the hooves of a hundred horses, and his face began to sweat. The king made the rounds of the sleeping men, and soon came to the groom."

The audience were thoroughly drunk by now. "And he skewered him on the spot," hollered a warrior.

"Dragged him outside to beat him, then slashed his throat," suggested another.

"He dispatched him to hell with one blow of his axe," called out a third.

"He did none of those things," said Egbert. "This king was too clever for that. He saw no need to act in haste. He reached for the dagger that hung from his belt and sliced off a chunk of the man's beard. When daylight came the king would know who had transgressed. He would deal with the culprit privately and avoid a scandal that would only serve to embarrass his innocent lady.

"But the groom was craftier than the king had anticipated," Egbert explained. "After the king left, the rascal took a knife off the wall and notched the beard of every man in the stable. It was the talk of the hall the next morning when the men assembled for the hunt.

"The king took a walk to mull over the situation. In the end, he thought, what had the fellow purloined? The king could not point to any missing thing. What he had had before, he had now. Perhaps it wasn't such a grave crime and, for the sake of his lady's equanimity, it would be best forgotten.

"The king gathered the stable hands together and made a little speech. 'Someone here has tasted wine he was not entitled to sip. I cannot allow a thief in our midst. As the good Christian I am, I will not hang him, but I expect him to confess to God and mend his ways. I also expect him to be gone before I return from the hunt this afternoon.'

"The stableboy, sad to leave his lover but thrilled to escape with his life, hastily departed for a distant land. He most likely got conscripted into a foreign army and, lacking skill, soon fell on the battlefield. In any case, no one ever heard of him again. The wise king ruled long and well, and his blameless, beautiful, and contented wife bore him many sons."

The warriors and their ladies seemed to enjoy this tale. The good prevailed, the bad banished: order had been restored. I laughed at the end like everyone else, maybe a little harder than warranted, and Egbert said, "I didn't think it was as funny as all that, my lady."

"My lord," I said, "I do enjoy a story where the woman bests the man."

He looked at me blankly; it was clear he hadn't puzzled out the real story. I elaborated. "Is there a woman so dim that she doesn't know the girth of her husband, the smell of his hair, how he tastes?"

"You're not thinking," said Egbert. "If she knew it wasn't her husband, why would she admit to having a lover when the king entered her bedchamber?"

"You'll remember her lover had just left when the king arrived. For all she knew he might have passed the groom in the hallway. It's possible her husband might have spotted a retreating figure—"

"And figured it out," said Egbert. "But no. I can't believe she knew her lover wasn't the king. A queen would not allow a lowly stable boy such liberties."

"You remember the king's dalliance with a chambermaid? Turnabout is fair play, my lord. We women have our pride."

"What's good for the goose?"

"And don't you forget it."

"But the king handled it well."

"You seem determined to think so, my lord."

"He showed self-restraint. There was no scandal. No blood flowed, and he rid himself of the troublesome fellow."

"Did he?"

"What?"

"You seem to have forgotten that the king went on a hunt that afternoon. With him out of the way, the stableboy sought out the queen to say goodbye. She gave him a purse stuffed with gold and sent him to be a gamekeeper on one of her estates. No one thought a thing about it when she visited her hunting lodge."

"Well," said Egbert, "At least she gave the king many sons."

"Yes," I agreed. "And most of them had a special affinity with horses."

The Vulture and the Raven

HOLLY TANNEN - WRITERS OF THE MENDOCINO COAST

A pair of turkey vultures roosted in a dead pine tree over looking Big River. The beach was littered with the bodies of unvaccinated tourists, so they feasted, and reared three chicks instead of their usual two.

But Fuddlehead's Cafe closed, the bikers left Mendocino, and the birds had to revert to their traditional fare of dead skunks, raccoons, and the odd labradoodle. The downy white chicks huddled together, waiting for Mom and Dad to return and re-gurgitate food for them. If a hawk circled overhead, Veronica, Violet, and Victor hissed like snakes and frightened it away.

One foggy day, their mother told them it was time they learned to hunt. Veronica, the eldest, took off first. She flew down the beach and found the carcass of a harbor seal. But, try as she might, she couldn't tear through the thick skin. She headed back to the pine tree, wet and dejected, and her mother had to dis-gorge dinner for her.

"Sissy," said Victor. "I could have opened that carcass with my mighty beak."

Then Violet set out on her first feeding flight. She scoped out Highway One until she came upon a dead cat. But whenever she settled down to eat, a log truck whizzed by, and she had to take wing. She flew home, cold and downhearted, and her mother regurgitated meat for her.

"Wuss," said Victor. "I'd have flapped my fearsome wings and scared off those trucks."

Then it was Victor's turn. He soared up Big River until he smelled a squashed skunk.

"I'll show those girls how to deal with carrion," he chortled. He glided down and landed next to the carcass. Tearing off bits of flesh, he gorged himself. Then he saw five black birds overhead. Ravens! Must be that Stanford bunch. They landed on the ground beside the skunk.

"Flock off," he hollered. "You get plenty of scraps at the Inn."

"Tofu gives me the runs," said a female raven. "And don't get me going about kale."

Rather than keeping a respectful distance, the ravens huddled close by. The female left the group and hopped past him. She's probably headed off to take a pee, Victor thought, as he tore through fur and skin into the skunk's insect-filled intestines. All of a sudden he felt a searing pain in his rear end. He whirled around and snapped at the raven, who jumped sideways and flapped into the air, *kworking*.

He chased her onto the topmost branch of a redwood tree. By the time he made his way back to the road, the other ravens had pulled the carcass under a blackberry bush and were daintily lunching.

He returned home, wings drooping, turning round and round the nest cavity in a vain attempt to hide his missing tail feathers. His mother preened his head. "Tomorrow your sisters will show you how to do it," she said. "Have some nice vomit."

The World to Him

JANE GLENDINNING - BERKELEY

Loose gravel rolled under my foot as I stepped from my pickup. Afraid of falling, I kept an eye on the path ahead and chose my steps with care. I pushed through the gate where four dogs played chase, dodging obstacles scattered in the dusty yard. Hans ran at the back of the pack, a giant Snoopy doll held in his jaw. His features, some mix of Labrador, and the grey tufts in his black coat displayed his age. His wild and happy eyes followed his playmates.

Someone who knew of my recent break-up had phoned me about this dog who needed a home. "He's seven and a half years old or so," she said. "His owner checked herself into rehab and will be away for months. She asked her friends to find him a new home. I thought of you right away, living alone for the first time in years." She paused and I kept silent. "You need a dog," she said.

I didn't need a dog and I didn't want a dog. I wanted to live my life so fast that the memory of my recent relationship would be a blur. I couldn't do that with a dog. Especially one almost eight years old. Abandoned by the person closest to him. For rehab. I did not want to take him, but I understood the need to move on. And I understood wanting to make your life better.

"If it doesn't work out, you can bring him back," she'd said. That's when I agreed to 'meet' him, knowing that meant 'take' him. Despite the promise, I knew I couldn't take him back because of what that would say about me, how easily I abandon. How I don't care.

Friends took sides in my recent break-up. I hid my misery from them while in the relationship. We were an active couple. People thought of her as sweet and fun while I felt badgered and belittled living with someone whose morals were in combat with mine. When I could not identify a shred of love for her, I left. Acquaintances reminded me that it is the villain who leaves.

Now, entering a new relationship with this dog that I did not want, I hoped for some feeling of redemption because of my good deed. I opened the camper shell, and with a heavy heart, watched Hans jump in. He still held the stuffed Snoopy between his teeth. His leash and an old curry comb, its handle so worn it would soon come apart, his only other belongings.

I lived on the second floor of a four-plex near Bernal Hill, and just above Precita Park. I thought Hans could do his business on the hard surface of the patio, easily accessed by a single flight of stairs outside my backdoor. He didn't agree with or understand my plan. He came from country living and only relieved himself on soil and plants, not on cement.

We walked the half block to the park. Hans cringed and lowered himself to the sidewalk at the shudder of a passing bus. I held his leash tight in case the noise made him bolt. We crossed Folsom Street and entered the grassy park. Hans rolled onto his spine and stretched himself into a back and forth wiggle. I wasn't sure if he was eager for the dirt or if he had an itch. His thick coat had that sticky feeling from needing a bath.

I kept his leash fixed to his collar and we travelled the length of the park, up and back and across a couple of times. Hans stayed attentive to my moves and did not pull away. I slid onto a bench and he lay at my feet, both of us looking off. I forgot how comforting a dogs' steady warmth against my leg could be. He had to be nervous with me, a new person, and in an unfamiliar place, but he held that life-loving, dog dignity and seemed to enjoy relaxing in the park.

When I shifted to pull my face out of direct sunlight, Hans raised his head and, looking at me, began rapidly wagging the very tip of his tail as though urging me to share a secret with him. I pushed the palm of my hand back across his forehead and scratched the scruff of his neck gently digging my fingers into the coarse fur. "Good dog, Hans," I said. He lay back, his tail thumping in the low grass.

Hans proved to be an easy dog to live with. He didn't want to sleep on my bed, but took his place on the floor. I did what I could to keep him comfortable. Dog-walkers took him out when my work days stretched into long hours. He ate good food, and every morning after his breakfast, we walked up the street and watched the sun rise over the East Bay hills. I tried to time things to not rush Hans, allowing him to sniff and explore. I could watch him from a bench or follow him as he gathered the world through his nose.

I knew I had a good dog, still my emotions were tangled. It was as though I fought loving him because if I loved him, I owed him. I could not stand the thought of owing my time and attention if I had to pretend it brought me pleasure. But things were okay, and I began to relax enough to think about having a bigger life with Hans in it. It was time to explore some of the other dog areas around San Francisco. I loaded Hans into my pickup and we rode across the city to Fort Funston.

I parked in the blacktop lot and leashed Hans before letting him out of the truck. He obediently heeled, and when the parking lot faded from view, I unhooked the lead from his collar. Hans put his head to the sandy path for a second and, without a glance my way, darted off across the vine-covered terrain and toward a wall draped in ice plant.

"Hans, come," I called, but he did not slow down, and I ran after him. He reached the wall and climbed the thick plants to the crest and then slipped out of sight. I knew that on the other side of that wall the precipice dropped to the shore of the Pacific Ocean.

I ran back, beyond the park entrance, to a path of wooden steps leading down to the beach. It felt like a long distance, my legs leaden crossing back through the sand to the cliffs, and though I wanted to find him, I dreaded what I might see.

The cliff loomed like a guardian of the ocean. Vines and the thick stems of small bushes protected the steep surface. I scanned the landscape in dread and pushed against a hardness in my chest to draw a breath. I still did not whole-heartedly want him, and he deserved more than that. He deserved a home, cherished as someone's absolute best dog in the world.

Two people faced the cliff, one of them pointing upward, the other shading her eyes. I hurried toward them and looking up saw Hans seek footing several feet below the crest. He appeared balanced among the old branches forty feet or so above the beach. The person pointing yelled over the sound of the waves, "Look at that dog."

"It's my dog," I said.

I did the only thing that made sense to me at that moment. I kept still and watched while Hans chose his steps with some eagerness and a great deal of thought. His body quivered and his feet danced, barely lifting from the surface until ready for his next move.

With each step he took, I thought he would tumble. My throat pinched, and I felt sick watching him. He faced the beach, his tail end above his shoulders. He appeared to find a spot wide enough to support one paw, but too narrow for the balance he needed. I watched him try to pull himself back. He pushed with both front paws against the short, thick stem of a low shrub, his weight shifted to his tail end. The ground moved below his hind paws, sand slid and pulled his rump further down the side. I thought he showed fear, but it was probably my own. He gripped and pulled himself steady with his front legs and found a stable perch to support his rear. Hans could see what I could not. His wrong move did not stop his journey. He did not look back toward the top as if wanting to retrace his way to safety. He studied the terrain in front of him and found his next move.

Hans' direct and clumsy route put him in this predicament. He continued on his way showing some impatience, but I could see how he geared his movements toward the safe attainment of what he wanted. His desire gave him reason to climb the vines and slip over the edge to find himself on this cliff. He took a risk and ran toward something that meant the world to him. He could go for it. On the cliff Hans became more of himself. He showed himself to be a better dog than I felt myself to be as a person.

He took a step downward, then traveled across the rocky mass away from me. I feared this meant he was stuck since he no longer aimed downward. But further away, he found a better route and crossed back toward my direction again on a path that brought him closer by a few more feet. Hans traveled back and forth across the bushes and the rocky surface until he came within ten feet or so of the beach.

He looked so happy, so excited. His body quivered more than before, practically a whole body wag, and his feet no longer looked tentative in their dancing. He lifted them in readiness. So close to the beach, seven or eight feet up, Hans skidded into a shrub and his weight pulled him through the branches. The rocky cliff curved outward and he landed on his side on the hard surface. I saw him look down. His legs straightened, and he began to slide again before partly running and partly jumping the last five feet.

He fell to the beach with a thud, his legs not holding him up under the momentum. I thought he was hurt, but before I reached him, he raised himself and took a quick, playful lunge at me, then turned and sped toward the breaking waves, ears blowing in the breeze, me far behind, both of us kicking sand in our wake.

Traditions

PRISCILLA COMEN - WRITERS OF THE MENDOCINO COAST

Christmas will be different this year. I won't go to lunch with my granddaughter Seidy at the Headlands Café as we have in the past. We won't cross Laurel Street to Pippi Longstocking's store to buy socks for my other two granddaughters. Pippi's is online now, and because restrictions and tensions rise as the number of Coronavirus cases increases, other stores allow only six customers at a time

There's more time to read since we're not going anywhere during these dangerous days. I'm reading a book about a young woman in Paris in the 1940s. The Nazis occupy the city. They are looking for Jews to ship off to the camps. The mood there is tense. The protagonist must keep a low profile, stay away from her papa's flower shop, and not go to lunch with her friends. She avoids getting too close to others on the street. During this pandemic, we also feel isolated. When walking in my small town, I see how many people are wearing masks, and take it personally if they're not.

It's funny how one's time of life can lead to thoughts of other days. Forty-five years ago while living in Malibu, we were invited to a friend's home on Christmas Eve to decorate their tree. The adults got drunk, and the children — their five and our three — ran around the big house eating the popcorn made to trim their eight-foot tree. Adam, their oldest son, made me a large vodka and orange juice drink, a Screwdriver. It went down easily, and after we returned home, my husband told me I was the "life of the party" as he hosed out the inside of our VW Bug. Those were the good old days when almost anything was okay.

This year we won't go to our daughter's on Christmas morning for a breakfast of lox and bagels. Nor will we stop by our son's house to give presents to his children. As old-timers at eighty-eight and ninety-eight, we are too vulnerable to infection. Instead, we might leave the gifts at the front doors of both families early in the morning, or the night before. The children may think Santa really did come to their homes. I hope so.

A tradition I will continue this year is setting the red-coated Santas around the living room and in the front of the picture window. My father used them in the 1950s to decorate the display windows of the sportswear shops where he worked. I will also hang a simple wreath on our front door and put a huge poinsettia plant on the coffee table in its place of honor.

Our street is lit every night from five until ten with decorative displays shining onto house fronts and colorful ornaments hanging from trees. The neighborhood is bright, and my heart is full. It's a joyous feeling that will soften the stories of Covid variants we hear at the grocery store and on news reports.

I will light the Chanukah candles for eight nights at sundown to commemorate the miracle in Jerusalem thousands of years ago. Although there was only enough oil to last for one night, the candles burned for eight days. Chanukah is a custom that endures for centuries, another tradition Jewish people have followed every year.

One evening as we finish our Dijon chicken, red and blue lights flash through the glass panes of our front door. We rush outside to see what the emergency is, and a red fire truck drives past with Santa Claus on top, wearing fuzzy red and white clothes with a wide, white belt. He waves his arms and throws candy canes to the children.

When I call my ten-year-old granddaughter Lily to tell her Santa was here, she says, "Get used to it. He comes every year."

Today I will make Russian tea cookies and Lily has arrived to help with the baking. She wears a mask, and we stay a good distance apart. Christmas tins wait to be filled and delivered to dear neighbors, the mail person, and my physical therapists.

"Happy Holidays" goes onto the labels and I check to be sure I have all the ingredients. The recipe says to mix them together in a bowl, roll into one-inch balls, set one inch apart on an ungreased cookie sheet, bake at 350 degrees for ten to twelve minutes, shake in a bag with powdered sugar then cool a long time and enjoy!

As Lily helps, she encourages me to add more sherry. "We'll get drunk," she says and giggles before tucking her straight, black hair behind her ears then rolling up the sleeves of her pink shirt. She's ready to go to work. "This smells like Christmas," she says before she scoops out the batter to form little balls.

My granddaughter was abandoned in China at the age of two but has grown into a happy child at peace with her American family and herself. I hope Lily and I will make Russian tea cookies for years to come. After all, it is a tradition.

Sandpipers

JILL EGLAND - WRITERS OF KERN

Pause motionless
ankle-deep in the sea
and soon they come
snippets of answers
to unspoken questions
scurrying on twig legs
at impossible speeds
heads bobbing in ancient
aerodynamic rhythm
barely displacing sand and water.

I don't know where they keep their families,
raise their babies.
All I know is that each dawn they
flock to the bay's edge
follow the waves
mimic its ebb
find what they seek
while I remain rooted
impervious to tidal patterns
as the water deepens.

At the end of the day
we sit on the sand
shoulders touching, sun behind us.
You point to the horizon.
"There's Portugal. Or maybe Madagascar."
The wind blows my response
westward. Away from you.
In front of us, sandpipers dance
a perfect choreography on a
changing shoreline.

Dimensional

JOAN OSTERMAN - NAPA VALLEY WRITERS

The empty chair dominates.
Mom—stolid—serves cinnamon
toast, cocoa, to her remaining child.

One day a baby girl, transplanted,
takes the place of the son
cut down by cancer.

The adopted daughter adapts,
shallows her breath, strains
against fibers of dreams

spun for her brother.
The parents swaddle her
in remnants of frayed hopes.

She grows upward, inward.
Wins at pick-up sticks
with her spider fingers.

Slips through the margin between
door and frame. Climbs a sapling,
perches on a pencil-thin branch.

Summer—Atlantic City. She wraps
willowy legs around a striped
yellow, red, blue beach ball,

rolls into the ocean, tumbles
in rough, salty waves—but the sea
returns her to warm sand.

Her big sister scoops her up,
brings her back to family,
shares pink cotton candy.

The parents ask their youngest,
"What do you want to become?
Teacher, Doctor, Scientist?"

"I want to be Dimensional.

To stretch to the sun, scrape
rainbows in the sky, thicken
my trunk, widen my crown,

harbor hundreds of songbirds.
Flutter my leaves in the breeze.
I want to flower and seed."

Invasive Plants

JEANNE RANA - BERKELEY

the mint pushes
against the sides of its pot
impatient caged
it will get rootbound
but won't die
it will be the domesticated herb
used for garnish
or a sprig in lemonade

the bamboo will have its way
stubborn   subversive
it will spring up
five feet down the path
jump a wall
I don't trust it at all

morning glory
I love the most
I want to crawl into
the deep blue flower
and drown
I'm always tempted
to plant it again
the same feeling
I used to have about
all the bad boys
I wanted

invasive plants
high maintenance
unlike subtle succulents
self-contained   modest
dare I say it?
boring

Werewolf versus Bananas

MIKE APODACA - HIGH DESERT

It all started in 1968, when I was in seventh grade. Batman—the Adam West version—had been all the rage on TV. My family had gathered in front of the set for two nights each week—never missing an episode.

And then it was cancelled.

My junior high held a costume contest, so, of course, I decided to bring back the magic and dressed up as the Caped Crusader. I wore tights, a dark blue bath-robe (cape), and a utility belt, complete with an Alka-Seltzer box. An uncomfortable thick plastic, helmet-like cowl topped off the whole ensemble. It took me days to gather it all, but it was worth it.

On my way to school, I jaywalked across Slauson Boulevard, a busy four-lane highway behind the school. I rushed into the middle of the street, put up my gloved hand, stopped traffic, and strutted away as only Batman can. I could swear I heard the dah-dah-da-da-dah-dah-da-da theme song in my ears.

Confident I'd win the contest, I put myself forward as a contender.

Imagine my surprise when I was beaten by a kid loosely wrapped in stringy toilet paper who said he was a mummy. He wasn't. The whole thing must have taken him two minutes to create.

The incident bothered me. I'd been robbed. Surely these judges didn't understand just how superior my rag-tag Batman was compared to this TP excuse for an interred Egyptian pharaoh. The unfairness of it all was like a rasp scraping my soul.

Fast forward four years. I focused on theater arts in high school and became quite adept at my craft, landing the lead in several plays and becoming the vice president of the school's drama department. My heart swelled when the Pioneer High School Student Council announced a Halloween dance with a costume competition. I decided this time I'd give my fellow students a performance they'd never forget. Vindication would be mine.

I invested in professional makeup and spent three hours getting into costume. I began my transformation by rubbing black greasepaint under my eyes and on the sides of my nose. Then I painted my fingernails with black nail polish. I painstakingly glued dark brown crepe hair (a fiber-based, yarn-like hair we used for beards and stuff on the stage) all over my face, neck, chest, and on the backs of my hands. A pair of vampire teeth cut in half gave me my bottom fangs. I donned a dark brown wig over my blond hair. The jeans I wore had a large hole, so I glued hair to my leg behind it. To top off my masterpiece, I locked a long chain to my right leg, giving the impression that I'd been restrained but had broken loose and escaped. The *pièce de résistance* was my growl. It was magnificent. I'd start with a sharp, guttural snarl followed by an explosive, hissing bark.

Because I was in costume a little early, I tried out my act. As dusk fell in my quiet tree-lined neighborhood, and kids started roaming in search of sweets, I hid in the bushes in front of my house. When the unwitting costumed victims approached, clambering up the concrete walk that led to our front door, I'd jump out, hunched over, chain clanging, snarl raging, claws swiping viciously. Children ran screaming, terrified out of their wits.

Perfection!

The high school gym thundered with loud music while hundreds of dancers scuffed up the wooden basketball floor. Most had on wild party hats or store-bought costumes. I entered alone, bent over, jumping at people, barking, and generally scaring everyone I could. Lon Chaney had nothing on me. People pointed in my direction. No one recognized me. They asked me who I was, but I stayed in character, answering with a vicious snarl.

They were lucky I didn't tear them to shreds.

And then the crucial moment came. The Master of Ceremonies, the student body president, announced the costume contest. He pointed at me and shouted into the microphone, "Let's bring up the Wolfman!" Students around me cheered. I roared and swiped all the way up to the stage. In front of the undulating crowd, I howled and barked like I wanted to kill them all.

The MC called nine or ten others to come up. I was joined by a long line of thrown-together clowns, a Raggedy Ann, a hobo, and some superheroes.

No competition at all.

"Our contest will be decided by you, the audience," the MC announced. "The loudest applause wins." He walked to the front of the line and put his hand above the clown. The applause was respectful, but tepid. Same for Wonder Woman, Raggedy Ann, and the others.

Then the hand hovered above my shaggy head. I went into a rage, lashing out toward the audience. Raucous applause filled the massive gym. There were cat calls and cheers. The crowd loudly chanted, "Wolfman! Wolfman!"

I had won! Years of humiliation melted away in the sweet satisfaction of victory. The world made sense once again.

And then the MC's hand lifted above the last contestant in line. It was actually two people. They'd taken yellow sheets and sewn them roughly into the shape of bananas and cut eye holes. Honestly, they looked more like yellow pointy-headed ghosts than bananas.

Although my applause had been substantial, this eruption of adulation was far more robust. The crowd went crazy, their shouts and cheers so loud it hurt my ears.

Absolutely perplexed, I tried to make sense of this. How could two poorly clad bananas, a costume that may have taken fifteen minutes to put together, have overcome my excellent lycanthrope? The bananas didn't act. They didn't parade around in character. They just stood there peering out of their off-centered eye holes. How could they possibly have beaten me?

Then the bananas shed their peels revealing the star football player—who had broken his leg in the big game the week before—and his cheerleader girlfriend. They were given a sizeable trophy to another round of thunderous applause.

It was at that moment that I discovered a profound life truth—it's not always the best that wins. Often there are other factors—mitigating circumstances and biases—that overshadow quality and superiority. It's just the way it is.

Learning this lesson has helped me greatly, although it was hard to appreciate it while I scraped myself raw trying to get all the crusty glue and stringy crepe hair off my aching skin.

When I arrived home, my mom showed me that the candy bowl by the front door was still full. Apparently word got out that there was a monster at our house, and kids decided it wasn't worth it to risk their lives for a paltry one-inch Snickers bar.

So, at least I ended up with a large bowl full of candy.

Where Have All My Nouns Gone?

LUCRETIA LEONG - SAN FRANCISCO PENINSULA

My nouns are stuck in Purgatory. Sometimes I wonder if the capricious gods are trying to embarrass me as I am left standing with my mouth hanging open with no nouns coming forth. Without these quintessential words at my fingertips, or on the tip of my tongue, I feel hampered. How can I be a charismatic conversationalist or a friendly passerby who just wants to socialize with others? What will it take to release my poor nouns from Purgatory? Would baptizing them with holy water work? Having command of my nouns again would be such a boost to my self-esteem.

Why the nouns? Especially the proper ones. Last week when I wanted to tell a friend about a movie, my jaw opened then closed because I couldn't remember the title. To save face, I took a slow breath as if the pause was deliberate and changed the subject to the excellent acting in the film. The actor's tortured face appeared before me, but his name evaporated like yesterday's rain drops. I felt like a bumbling idiot. Only after we left the restaurant and went our separate ways did I remember it was the actor Ethan Hawke, the minister in the movie *First Reformed*.

It's not only the titles of movies or the names of objects and famous people that I can't recall. Another time at dinner, I began addressing a good friend, but her name suddenly vanished down a rabbit hole. My wise friend chuckled as she saw the sudden look of alarm on my face. Thank God she was not offended; this dear friend who fondly sends me care packages from Hawaii, emails me daily, and comes to visit me in California. And I couldn't remember her name! Even my family is not exempt from my noun-losing affliction. I often call my older son Jonathan and my younger son Kevin which is a reversal of their names. They too, good-naturedly, are not offended and accept my *faux pas* as a consequence of their mother getting old and harebrained.

But it's not just the proper nouns that I'm losing. Common nouns have also been relegated to Purgatory. The "ottoman" slips from under me, leaving my bare feet to fall on the cold floor, the "leaf blower" with its loud, boisterous rumblings blows away its own nomenclature, and the "deck scrub brush" is brusquely removed from memory.

I have deduced that it is definitely a noun problem. I have no problems remembering the other major parts of speech: adjectives, adverbs, verbs, and prepositions. They all leap forward with *panache* and sail blissfully into fulfillment. Adjectives are *ponderous, eloquent, flamboyant, expressive, dynamic,* and *memorable.* Staunch adverbs march forth *boldly, effortlessly, worldly, gladly and solidly* onto new terrains. Verbs appear in full regalia; they *saunter, leap, frolic, romp, cavort, and augur* upon the dance floor of life. And prepositions leap out *from, under, behind, above, around,* and *across* with great aplomb.

On a serious note, my subconscious has always worried about these purgatorial nouns. This condition has been ongoing for a while, maybe a dozen years or more. It doesn't seem to be worse (hopefully not), but it worries me. Sinking into the sofa in a dim corner of my living room, I ruminate on the state of my brain. I often scare myself into thinking I'm experiencing the early stages of dementia or Alzheimer's. With my trusty iPad before me, I decide to do some research. The volumes of encyclopedias that used to sit on my bookshelf have been replaced by my mobile devices. Instead of thumbing through pages, my fingers do the walking on a touch screen where I delve into the wonderful world of hyperlinks.

On the internet, I discover that my malady could be a condition known as anomic aphasia where a person who maintains speech fluency, comprehension, and syntax has difficulty in word finding. Another condition called semantic dementia targets the loss of nouns. As I dig deeper into the layers of my unfathomable online search, I become anxious; I identify with all the symptoms that I encounter. I begin to see this loss of nouns as the beginnings of a serious memory problem. Hypochondria sprouts her wings and takes flight as I imagine myself wandering the streets of Burlingame, California, not knowing how to get home. Or bouncing down Highway 101 at 70 miles per hour, and suddenly forgetting where I'm going. I'm in a dark forest *à la* Hansel and Gretel *sans* breadcrumbs. I'm in tears and a complete bundle of nerves!

"Stop it," I cry out, "get a grip on yourself. This isn't impossible; I can do something about this!"

There are mnemonic habits I could practice. If I meet someone named Miles, I will remember the exhilarating music of Miles Davis, and if a woman's name is Jennifer, I'll call to mind Jennifer Lopez in all her curvaceous glory. Whenever I watch a movie, I must make a point to impress its title and actors upon my cerebral cortex. I will be attentive and not just gloss over any name or title with nary a second thought.

Perhaps this lack of specificity can be explained by my being born, raised and living most of my life in Hawaii. Hawaiian pidgin English likes to cut corners and not bother with wordiness. It's okay to talk a lot, but it's not okay to be wordy. Everything is *like dat* or *ova dare* or *da kine,* or *whatchamacallit.* It is a culture of not needing to be specific in naming objects and people. This shortcut of language may not have served me well in my golden years. Of course, I am aware that the blame may not be on my cultural heritage, but may rest on my own shoulders. Regardless, I have no choice but to marshal my precious nouns around me and forge ahead with mindfulness.